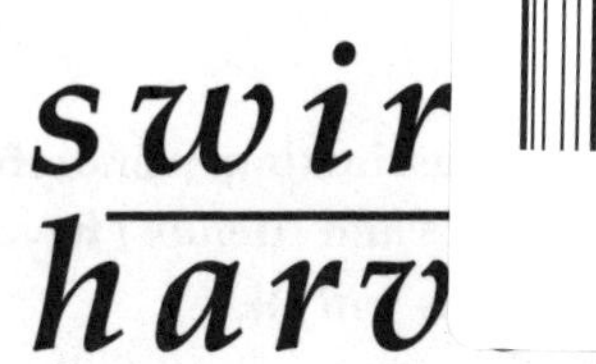

views from the CROP CIRCLE frontline

ANDY THOMAS

Illustrated & designed by

ALLAN BROWN

This book is dedicated to all the fascinating, wonderful (and occasionally infuriating) cerealogical colleagues and friends I have had over the years. Bless 'em all.

First published in 2003 by Vital Signs Publishing and S B Publications
VSP: 13 Downsview Cottages, Cooksbridge, East Sussex, BN8 4TA
SBP: 19 Grove Road, Seaford, East Sussex, BN25 1TP

Design & layout by Allan Brown

2A Crescent Road, Brighton, East Sussex, BN2 3RP
darroch@dircon.co.uk

ISBN 1-85770-272-7

Other books by Andy Thomas:

Fields of Mystery: The Crop Circle Phenomenon in Sussex
Quest For Contact: A True Story of Crop Circles, Psychics and UFOs (with Paul Bura)
Vital Signs: A Complete Guide to the Crop Circle Mystery and Why it is NOT a Hoax
A Oneness of Mind: The Power of Collective Thought and Signs of Our Times
Streets of Fire: A Hymn to Lewes and the Bonfire Celebrations
The Lewes Flood (charity flood relief book)
An Introduction to Crop Circles (as editor)

Printed by Antony Rowe Ltd
Bumper's Farm Ind Est, Bristol Road, Chippenham, Wilts, SN14 6LH
01249 659705

CONTENTS

ACKNOWLEDGMENTS

Andy Thomas would like to express deep gratitude to the following people:

Allan Brown for his intrepid design work, willingness and dedication; *Catherine MacNaughton* for her proofing skills, invaluable friendship and brutal honesty; *Sir Laurence Gardner* for his generous foreword and help with the white dust piece; *Rodney Ashby, Jim Lyons* and *Marcus Allen* for *their* useful help with the dust article; *Geoff Stray* and *Jack Sullivan* for help with the galaxy article; *Jason Porthouse* for design advice and image capturing; *Michael Glickman* and *Andreas Müller* for additional diagrams; *Dave 'Griller' Gilgannon* for being the cover star; All the skilled photographers featured in the book; All my crop circle friends and colleagues, including everyone at *Swirled News, the Glastonbury Symposium* and *Southern Circular Research; Lindsay Woods* and *Steve Benz* at S B Publications for continuing faith; and, of course, *Kaye Thomas* for love and understanding beyond the call of duty.

Thank you all.

FOREWORD

By Sir Laurence Gardner

During the 16th century, King Henry VIII became interested in th
customs of rural England and sent his antiquary, John Leland, on a fa
finding tour. In the course of this, Leland asked the people of Wesse
about their village-green ring dances. "They are so intricate," h
exclaimed; "how on earth do you devise such complex routines?" Th
answer surprised him. "We base them," came the reply, "on the mag
grass designs which appear in our fields."

On learning this, I was no less surprised than the antiquary, for h
was first-hand documentary evidence of crop circles from over 470 y
ago. Clearly, they are not phenomena of our modern age, as so m
people suppose. Such documented records do not explain the natu
origin of agriglyphs, but they do provide proof of their histo
provenance as subjects of past fascination.

Although I have attended, and spoken at, many crop circle confer
I have never considered myself to be a qualified cereologist as such
is mainly because so many others are light-years ahead of me i
related studies. I do, however, have numerous friends in the fra
who keep me abreast of annual occurrences. Consequently, I hav
than a passing interest in the subject and my research into ma
superconductivity, paramagnetism, flux tubes and hyper-dimens
led me to theorise a little about crop circles in recent times.

The prevailing question seems always to be: which crop circles are real, and which are hoaxes? In practical terms they are, of course, all real in that a forged painting is still a real painting even though a fake based on an original theme. The better question would be, therefore: which crop circles are of unknown origin, as against those which are man-made?

In this regard, opinions differ - often considerably - with the percentages falling heavily one way or the other. Unfortunately, press and media reporting does little to help the identification process, generally presenting audiences with the impossible task: "Decide for yourselves"! Enthusiasts, often with limited resources, are therefore left to make their own speculative judgements, with mainstream scientists totally ignoring the remarkable attributes of these awesome creations of unknown origin.

In *Swirled Harvest*, Andy Thomas takes an objective look at the pros and cons of the crop circle debate - approaching the subject headlong through a series of intriguing articles and anecdotes. The great value of this book, for croppies and novices alike, is that there is no hint of vested interest here. *Swirled Harvest* is not designed to influence the reader towards anything but a recognition that crop circles of unknown origin are more than worthy of an academic appraisal, which they have so far not been afforded. Whether discussing crop circles, the film *Signs*, or the Millennium Dome, Andy's well-balanced approach is honest, forthright and, above all, entirely compelling.

Laurence Gardner
Exeter, April 2003

Sir Laurence Gardner is the internationally acclaimed author of many books exploring holy bloodlines and the powers of ancient cultures, including Bloodline of the Holy Grail, Genesis of the Grail Kings *and* Realm of the Ring Lords.

INTRODUCTION

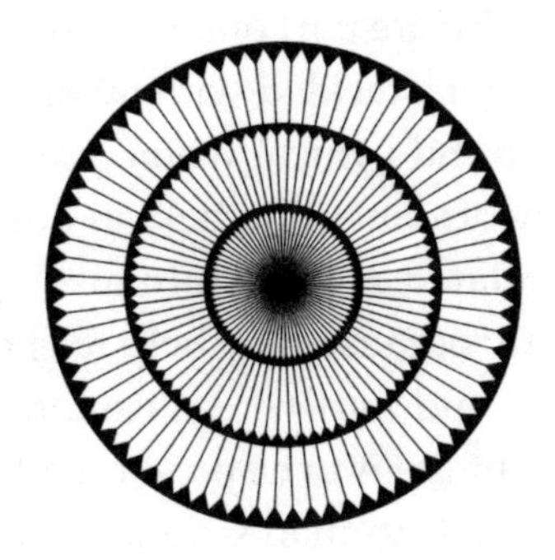

I have previously written three books exploring aspects of the crop circle phenomenon, most prominently *Vital Signs: A Complete Guide to the Crop Circle Mystery and Why it is NOT a Hoax*. That volume, I am happy to say, has become for many people the definitive book on the subject. *Vital Signs* was an attempt to furnish the reader with as many background facts, theories and photographic records of this extraordinary enigma as was possible, without causing overload, to show that here was something the sceptics could never entirely explain. But, inevitably, there were certain qualities and sides to the world of 'cerealogy', as the study of crop circles is known, that there just wasn't the room or remit to explore. Now is the chance!

Swirled Harvest is not a sequel to *Vital Signs*, but rather its sideways cousin. If you've never read a crop circle book before, there's enough here to fill in some of the basics (especially the first chapter), but the main function of this collection of pieces is to take you deep into the actual culture of the circular research arena as seen from the inside. It is not a visual or technical book on the subject (that's *Vital Signs*), nor does it argue in detail again for the reality of the phenomenon, which is taken as a given here, though the reader may note a continually defensive tone against the sceptics.

The subtitle *Views from the Crop Circle Frontline* indicates that not only does this book record some choice samples of the inside dealings of the research community and some of its colourful characters and events, but it also concerns how those who are part of it view the world outside, a world (especially through the media, tackled with aplomb here) which can often come across as predatory and cynical when one is trying desperately to wave a flag for the reality of something held in doubt by so many.

A number of other related subjects are also discussed amongst the cerealogical content, partly because they help to show where the circles sit in relation to other areas, and partly because they are unlikely to find a home elsewhere, but I want them to be preserved for posterity!

Rather than it being the lazy man's option, there is no better way to convey the ins and outs of living the crop circle experience than by this collection of essays and pieces written by me over a ten year period for a number of credited sources and journals, although the majority of them come from the long-running publication *SC* (originally *Sussex Circular*), which I edited from its start in 1992 to its closure and transference to the *Swirled News* website in 2001. The value of these pieces lies in that they are first-generation imprints of events, thoughts and feelings experienced *at the time*, and cover a number of developments and situations, some of them usefully archetypal, some of them historically significant, and some of them simply included to show the glorious absurdity of it all. There is also one brand new piece - *Dust to Dust* - written especially for this book. This mix from the years does mean there is some variation in the writing style (though by and large the pieces are presented chronologically), and the prose sometimes goes places I wouldn't necessarily go now, but, with just some editing and a few additions, I have tried to preserve the original text as much as possible. Where later events impinge or change anything, I have inserted the odd italicised note, and brief introductions to the pieces explain their context.

Sit back, then, and take a ride into the wonderful, strange and sometimes mad world of crop circles and beyond...

Andy Thomas

1 A CONCISE GUIDE TO CROP CIRCLES

Here, as a starter, are some basics for those unfamiliar with the crop circle phenomenon (those wishing to know the full story are advised to read my book Vital Signs*)... This piece was written as a concise guide for the general public and has appeared in various guises over the years. It has been oft-quoted - and sometimes liberally 'lifted' without permission! - but here it is in its complete form. More advanced readers can skip this atypical entry for the book and move onto the next piece if they wish, but reminding oneself of the origins and facts of the mystery is always a good exercise...*

Huge, complex and beautiful patterns are being found swirled into crop fields around the world every year. Their origin and purpose remains a complete mystery. Despite attempts to dismiss them as the work of human artists, some believe the evidence points to a much stranger explanation. Wherever they come from, these spectacular designs often display very clear symbolism, scientific, esoteric and astronomical, and demonstrate some extraordinary unexplained effects.

What are crop circles?

Crop circles - crop formations, crop patterns, crop glyphs, agriglyphs, corn circles, call them what you will - are geometrical areas of flattened plants, neatly laid into fields with often intricate qualities and little apparent damage to the stems. They are mostly laid in spirals, clockwise or anticlockwise, but sometimes crop is laid radially from the centre. Other directions and types of flow have been noted. The circle is the most common and basic component of a crop formation, but many other shapes are often incorporated. A combination of circles of various sizes and positionings, together with the additional complimentary configurations, go to make up the astonishing designs seen each year.

How many appear?

Around 250 crop designs around the world appear annually on average. Figures vary slightly from year to year, up and down. Several thousand have been documented since records began.

Where do they appear?

Crop circles are a global phenomenon, but predominantly appear in the Northern Hemisphere, with southern England as the main centre of activity, particularly Wiltshire. England has played host to around two-thirds of the recorded formations so far, but places as diverse as Germany, Canada, North America, The Netherlands, The Czech Republic and Russia, to name but a few, have also recorded many appearances.

When do they arrive?

Off-season formations do sometimes occur, but by and large they begin to appear from spring onwards until early autumn, with most arriving during the three main summer months of any given country.

What crops do they appear in?

Any crop can be a potential target for the phenomenon: wheat, barley and oilseed rape (canola) are the most commonly affected varieties in England, being the main crops grown, but formations have also been reported in rye, oats, flax, peas, potatoes, carrots, sweetcorn maize and many other mediums, including rice paddies in Japan. Formations have also been found in wild grass, bracken and other undergrowth-type plants.

How large are crop circles?
Size can vary from circles of just a foot or so across ('grapeshot'), to designs covering many hundreds of feet.

History
When two retired English pranksters, Doug Bower and Dave Chorley, claimed in 1991 to have invented the crop circle phenomenon as a joke a decade or so earlier, they couldn't have been aware that almost 300 documented formations predated their alleged exploits. Reports go back centuries and a seventeenth century illustration even shows the figure of the Devil creating what certainly looks like the type of marking in fields which began to attract serious attention from the 1980s onwards.

Swirled into growing crops, these circular indentations of carefully flattened stems looked at first like the result of freak whirlwinds. Some were a few feet across, but others were the size of tennis courts. It wasn't long before the appearance of symmetrical patterns and other unusual variations began to throw the weather theories into doubt.

By the late 1980s, rapidly increasing numbers and seemingly evolving designs, still based largely on circles, had begun to capture the public imagination. Tantalised by reports of glowing lights and other bizarre phenomena associated with the circles, everyone, from UFO buffs to eminent scientists, was trying to unravel the mystery.

In 1990, the arrival of 'pictograms', long symbolic chains of circles, rectangles and rings gave the crop circles their place in history. Newspapers and television channels eagerly reported these astonishing patterns. But the claims of Doug and Dave and other supposed hoaxers soon left the media disillusioned. Despite this, crop formations continue to be discovered in designs of growing sophistication and size which leave many convinced that there is an unexplained force at work.

Theories and Evidence

There has been intense debate over the circles' origins. Some believe they are communications from extra-terrestrials, pointing to the many sightings and videos of aerial phenomena seen in connection with crop formations. Others feel the lights may be the properties of an unknown natural energy which produces complex ground patterns. Others still have cited everything from Mother Earth to nature spirits being responsible. Experiments with the power of the mind have suggested it is possible to influence the creation of certain shapes, leading some to believe psychic forces are involved.

Beyond this, most other popular explanations for the crop circles have revolved around human activity, either involving satellite technology or, more usually, the simple actions of pranksters and landscape artists. However, in demonstrations, human teams have struggled to reproduce designs as geometrically complex as many seen in the fields, or have taken long hours to produce anything approaching them. Certain formations have been shown to have appeared within very short periods of time; the geometrical calculation and construction required for some simply could not be carried out in one night. Biological anomalies and unreproducable effects such as nodal bending (where stem nodes are bent at strange angles to create certain shapes in the lay - not possible by hand) are always absent from man-made designs.

Some of the patterns have shown breathtaking symbolic qualities. In 1994, for instance [*see chapter 15*], several galaxy-shaped glyphs displayed a conjunction of planets over the star constellation Cetus as it would be in April 2000, and in 1995 an accurate diagram of the Earth's inner solar system was discovered. However, despite these few shapes which appear to denote dates and astronomical conjunctions, most others remain obscure and are open to interpretation, seeming to reflect multi-cultural symbolism.

Work by laboratories on circle-affected crop has shown biological changes taking place at a cellular level, suggesting the involvement of microwave energy. Other physical tests have shown anomalies not yet replicated by man-made experiments. These, together with the lights, eye-witness accounts, reports of malfunctioning electronic equipment and health effects on people visiting circles, suggest the phenomenon should be looked at far more closely.

Whether the crop formations are warnings, messages of greeting or abstract doodles remains to be seen. As they amaze and frustrate in equal measure with their stunning beauty, no doubt they will continue to create further controversy. Even within the crop circle research community itself, there has been much intense debate, disagreement and division - but also much positivity and inspiration, sparked by the deep questions raised and by the simple influence of beauty in people's lives.

Circular Stories, Facts and Figures

Eye-witnesses: There are around two dozen eye-witness accounts of crop circles forming. All describe similar events; an invisible force coming out of nowhere in otherwise calm conditions and spinning the crops down within seconds, usually with surprising violence - yet little damage is found in the laid crop. Tornado-like funnels, light phenomena and high-pitched whistling sounds have also been reported.

Quick on the draw: In July 1996, a 915 feet spiral of 151 circles appeared in full view of the busy A303 road, opposite England's ancient monument Stonehenge, Wiltshire, within a 45 minute period one Sunday afternoon. A pilot, gamekeeper and security guard confirmed it had not been there before 5.30pm - yet shortly after 6.00pm, the massive formation was being spotted by passing tourists. Much smaller man-made designs have taken several hours to complete. This also disproves the myth that all crop circles appear by night.

Longest crop formation: This occurred at Etchilhampton, Wiltshire, in 1996 - a chain of circles and pathways approximately 4100 feet long crossed from one end of a field to another.

Largest design and most circles in one formation: The record for both these qualities is currently held by the huge motif at Milk Hill, Wiltshire, August 12th 2001 - 409 small circles made up a staggering six-armed design of around 800 feet diameter.

Largest expanse of laid crop in one design: A seven-petalled mandala which appeared in 1998 at Alton Barnes, Wiltshire, contained a single flattened area covering 6000 square metres.

Most geometrically perfect formation: Most would agree that the 1996 formation at Windmill Hill, Wiltshire, takes this award - an endless procession of perfect equilateral triangles, from large to small, could be drawn by overlaying geometrical shapes onto a triple-armed spiral of 194 circles covering an area of around 450 feet diameter. If just one of the main circles or arms had been even slightly misplaced, this geometry would not have worked.

Most visited formation: Stonehenge, 1996 (see *Quick on the draw* above) - it is estimated around 10,000 people entered this pattern once it was opened to the public by the farmer, partly through being so visible next to such a major landmark.

Most publicised formation: Alton Barnes, 1990 - many global newspapers and TV stations reported the appearance of this, the first of the large pictograms.

Most pictorial formation: Although most crop designs remain ambiguous and open to interpretation, a few have been clearly identifiable, not least those which actually depict known visual imagery, as with the 'face' formations. In 2001, a humanoid face rendered in pixels appeared (alongside a rectangular binary code) next to a radio telescope at Chilbolton, Hampshire. A year later, at Crabwood, near Winchester, Hampshire, a sequel to this arrived in the shape of a classic ET creature, this time rendered in thin scanning lines, holding out a disc of binary code. Such clearly pictorial glyphs remain the exception, however.

Scientific tests: Work by W C Levengood, a respected Michigan-based biophysicist, has shown notable biological changes taking place inside circle-laid stalks, which could be attributable to some kind of microwave energy. No man-made demonstration formation has ever produced these results, yet the majority of the hundreds of crop circles sampled have proved positive in this regard. Levengood's papers have been published in scientific journals and his work has been replicated by other laboratories working with the US-based BLT Research organisation. In 1995, tests on crop formation soil samples were conducted by ADAS, a division of the English Ministry of Agriculture. Although preliminary, they showed distinct anomalies in the nitrogen/nitrate ratios which could not be explained [*see chapter 6*]. There have been other scientific tests carried out by different bodies over the years, which have detected peculiar unexplained qualities.

Strange effects: There have been many reported effects on people's health, sometimes cures, sometimes ailments, which have come on while within crop circles. Animals sometimes behave strangely in crop formations. Electronic and mechanical equipment, videos, cameras and even combine harvesters have also been known to malfunction in odd ways, far above the average one would expect from chance.

Beliefs

As yet, there is a resistance to mass acceptance of the crop formations as anything other than a man-made joke, despite all the evidence pointing in another direction for at least a proportion of the glyphs. To accept that crop circles come from beyond physical human realms means reassessing many things accepted as 'normality'. It means taking seriously the big question of what or who is making the patterns. Some believe we already have enough evidence to have reached that point, but the general public seems happier to treat the phenomenon as harmless art. Those who make our rules for us also seem to prefer it that way. Many others feel, however, that the circles are heralds of some major changes for our planet and civilisation, marking either a tumultuous era of upheaval or some kind of spiritual renaissance.

Whatever the truth, there is no doubt the crop circles have left an indelible mark upon our culture, inspiring with their visual beauty and mystery, and have profoundly affected many people's lives...

Original article first written 1996, and adapted, updated and rewritten for several sources several times since!

2 WAITING FOR REG

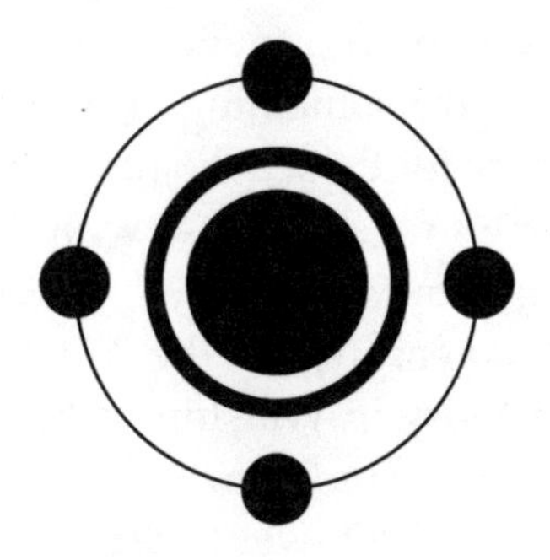

It's easy to forget the wide-eyed innocence of coming anew to the charming and treacherous world of cerealogy. The following piece, a diary of a few days spent in the Wiltshire circle heartlands in 1992, just a year after my first discovery of the phenomenon, attempts to capture this spark. The constant excitement at what might lie around the corner is tangible in every paragraph. Note that my poor wife was at this point still actually being dragged around by me on these trips before eventually becoming an honorary life member of the Crop Circle Widows society. This was the first season to follow the Doug and Dave hoax claims, and the resulting and, in retrospect, largely unjustified paranoia and doubt which gripped the scene at the time underlies the narrative, though I'm proud that even by then I was sounding appropriately suspicious of certain assertions. That said, these were still times when some of us would spend a night out in the freezing cold on the say-so of a retired rock star...

Reading someone's holiday diary is rather like looking at their holiday snaps; the novelty wears off quickly, the pictures are invariably blurry and only mean something to those who were there. However, the following account of a week spent circle-spotting and Silbury-watching in Wiltshire, while not quite guiltless of the above, may be worth reading a) because of information contained therein that may be of interest, and b) it may give something of the atmosphere in the world centre of crop circle activity for those who haven't experienced it.

Martin Noakes and entourage, together with Debbie Pardoe and Nigel Tomsett, like myself and my wife Kaye, chose the week beginning Monday 20th July 1992 to venture into the 'Wessex Triangle' (the 30-mile area centring around Avebury in Wiltshire, where the majority of global crop circle activity has occurred) partly to see if certain channelled predictions of spectacular UFO events around the ancient mound of Silbury Hill, as trumpeted by ex-rock star and circle enthusiast Reg Presley [*often used as a TV spokesman due to his celebrity, though he is today sceptical about most crop formations*], would come true on the 21st, and partly just to get a feel of the phenomenon this summer...

MONDAY 20 JULY

Kaye and I are driving to Wiltshire via Winchester. As we progress west, the skies grow steadily darker. On the A272, we reach Cheesefoot Head, site of so many crop circles in years past, and I pull up next to the 'Devil's Punchbowl' field to look at the (allegedly hoaxed) rings reported to be there - incredibly, no other formations have been reported in this area. As I get out to look, the heavens open and I realise that the field has been harvested anyway. Now rather damp, we drive on. Nothing at Chilcomb either. Not very promising.

We get onto the A34 to Newbury and spot our first formation, if fleetingly - it's the Sutton Scotney circle, the first event to be reported this year. It's looking a bit tired, but at least it's visible; that is until Kaye forces me to look at the road again. She doesn't want to die yet and certainly not on the A34.

5.00pm, Marlborough. We're here at last and, having dumped our luggage at our B&B hostel in Winterbourne Monkton (near Avebury), I've considered the looming weather and decided I need rather more robust shoes for the week. I'm just making my purchase when I spot Debbie and

Nigel in the street outside. I call out to them, giving the sales assistant a bit of a turn - she's had a long day and can probably do without cranks like me. We rush out and talk excitedly. They're camping a few miles away and I don't envy them, as several million gallons of water suddenly descend from the sky with a great clap of thunder. Nice weather for ducks. We see some ducks in a park on our drenched way back to the car. They seem to be enjoying themselves...

TUESDAY 21 JULY

At breakfast we meet three male German cerealogists who are staying at our B&B for the week. They seem pleasant but cagey when I tell them I'm a member of the Centre for Crop Circle Studies (CCCS). They're crop-watching at Alton Barnes and won't tell me an awful lot about what they're doing, but they have flown around the area in a hired light aircraft. Their pilot has told them that his plane always judders whenever he flies over a real crop formation, therefore if no juddering occurs when crossing one, it obviously isn't genuine. The Germans have taken this as the gospel litmus test. Very scientific. I ask if they have seen the pictogram we spotted last night, overlooking Avebury? Yes they have, but it must be a hoax because the plane didn't judder... Hmmm.

Later, I learn more about our German friends from the landlady of our hostel (who, of course, shouldn't really be telling me anything about them, but as I'm a CCCS member, etc.), who tells us that they consider the crop circles to be messages from the 'Second Solar System' and have come over to Britain (like last year) and created man-made 'replies' on land at the Carson farm in Alton Barnes (with permission). They are now out every night watching the skies for a response to their formations, which supposedly direct the aliens to a meeting at Silbury Hill (ah! - maybe our luck at Silbury tonight may be in). They appear to consider their man-made pictograms a great secret, which is rather a shame as they've made a diagram of them in the B&B Visitors' Book in the 'comments' column, obviously thinking them so cryptic that no-one would ever look twice [*the two main ringleaders, Joachim Koch and Hans-Jurgen Kyborg, went on to perform annual 'communication' experiments with man-made formations and would soon become openly known for their work*]. They have, of course, reckoned without me. Naturally, I do the decent thing and snaffle the Visitors' Book into our room to make a copy of the sketches, just for the record, you know.

This morning, Kaye and I decide to do a recce around Silbury Hill. The gods smile and glorious sunshine floods down, leaving my face beetroot red for the rest of the week. We are astonished by some of the wind damage in fields nearby - some of it is so flat and swirled that it wouldn't look out of place in an actual formation. It seems most unnatural, so I take some photographs. We and others we speak to notice a lot of this as the week progresses - some fields entirely flattened, other adjacent ones, of the same crop, untouched. I know this sometimes occurs, for mundane reasons as it were, but I've never seen it to this degree. Could this be some kind of connected but chaotic circle-making force at work in the field?

We climb Silbury Hill [*this was before a tourist-discouraging hole appeared in the top in 2000*] and meet a man from Holland up there. We talk about crop circles. Two very dubious-looking formations are visible either side of the mound - disappointing. Two figures suddenly appear, ascending the hill. It's Martin and his friend 'Griller' Gilgannon, searching for the lens Martin lost from his glasses the night before (amazingly, later they find it). Martin doesn't think the Avebury pictogram looks very convincing. We wonder what might happen up here tonight, the date for Reg's prediction... We'll be back to see.

To Avebury next, to have a closer look at the formation there. We stop for lunch first and bump into Debbie and Nigel again; they don't think much of the pictogram either and I have to admit it doesn't look too hot from a distance, but we'll see. Kaye and I head off to investigate. It's a £1.00-a-head-entry job, so into the field we go. My first impression is that it must be quite old, as it's very worn at the edges. Two long dumbbells are connected to each other by a rather wobbly-looking path. Silly embellishments have been made to it very roughly by people and it looks like they fell into the standing crop in the process. Despite this, however, it seems to me to be good. I lift a few layers of wheat and, with my basic humble knowledge, look for signs of authenticity, which seem to be there despite being the crop being well trodden. If this is a hoax, it's certainly a good one. At one end of the formation is a ring with a circle of standing crop in the middle. To my horror and anger, two American visitors let their children run right through the centre of it, smashing it down. I can't contain myself and complain to them. They just laugh. . . No wonder formations don't stay pristine for long. As we leave the field, the lady at the caravan tells us the formation is only three days old! Did we speak to the Canadian 'expert' we just passed, she asks, referring to a pony-tailed guy with a tape measure? We hadn't, but one thing I learnt this week is that anyone with a tape measure is considered to be an 'expert' around here. We see a lot of 'experts' in the next few days. I, obviously a mere novice, omitted to bring a tape measure with me, failing to see what good it does every individual measuring the same formations over and over again. Perhaps we should set up a 'Measurements and Dimensions' central information pool? [*Various organisations would eventually do this.*]

In the next field along, in amongst the wind damage, we spot three very rough but clear rings in a row, too regular surely to be weather-made, so we ask the lady if she knows anything about them. She hasn't even noticed them. A hoax or more strange wind damage?

After an afternoon's fruitless search at Barbury Castle for formations we learn are actually at Overtown Farm up the road, it's time to make our way to Silbury for the possible 'big event'... We meet Martin, Nigel and Debbie at the *Red Lion* pub in Avebury at 7.00pm as arranged. Martin's brought his partner Sloane along, together with friends Griller and Jo and two dogs to go with Nigel and Debbie's - we'll be well protected tonight, at least. Martin's been talking with a heavily-bearded American who is sitting outside the pub. He comes over and recounts to us how he saw a strange cloud over Silbury today, which took on the form of the sword and shield of the archangel Michael... Earlier on, Martin says this chap was smoking dope. Still, bearing in mind what we are about to do, we can hardly accuse him of crankiness...

At about 9.00pm, we take the footpath to Silbury Hill and select a footbridge over a dried up River Kennett as our viewing point for the night. There before us is the ancient mound, as silent and mysterious as ever, giving nothing away. It's rather excitingly like a boy scout field trip - Nigel's brought some canvas ground sheets. And so we settle down to our expectant vigil. Martin, Griller and I walk on to take a look at the car park - if no-one's there it doesn't bode well for anything happening tonight. In fact, there are quite a few vehicles parked up, and a couple of tents pitched, with people hanging around as if waiting for something. Clearly we're not the only ones here about to spend a night in hope. No sign of Reg Presley though...

Back at base camp, we quickly settle into a routine of patiently sitting or pacing the footbridge, scanning the skies, speculating amongst ourselves. It's a beautiful evening and the stars look wonderful as Silbury becomes a looming silhouette against the gentle glow of the sky. The night progresses and we see some incredibly bright shooting stars, but nothing more until... Suddenly there are lights bobbing about at the foot of the hill, moving to the summit! Hold on... They're torches - three or four people are climbing the mound. Is this Reg and crew preparing for the big event? They reach the top and stay there for a couple of hours. Nothing happens. By this time the girls are huddled up on the ground with the dogs, dozing fitfully, but by now it's too damp and cold to really get comfortable. A sudden cry of "Bastards!" from the hill is seemingly directed at the sky - why, we never discover, though frustration at the non-appearance of a spectacular lightshow might just be something to do with it. This seems to mark a watershed in our vigil, the thought dawning that nothing is going to happen tonight. No strange shapes in the sky, no figures of fire bursting from the hill. I do, however, see a strange light that moves in a series of slow jerks towards the horizon, but it doesn't last long and I don't mention it, as I am standing away from the others and am not sure about what I am seeing. (Reading an account later of 'jerky' lights over Barbury Castle in the book *Ciphers in the Crops*, this incident seems more significant, making me regret my silence.)

It's after three now and it'll be getting light soon. I'm quite prepared to stay for longer, but it is very cold and the girls, largely dragged here by the male obsessives, aren't happy. Sloane's voice floats up from the darkness: "Martin, I'm leaving you". We get the hint. Kaye's stomach's not feeling too good either, so we decide to call it a night. No-one needs any further prompting and we all pack up together, disappointed but somewhat relieved at the prospect of getting out of the damp night air. Perhaps we should have tried Alton Barnes...

WEDNESDAY 22 JULY

Surprisingly sprightly after almost no sleep, Kaye and I head off for Lockeridge and Alton Barnes. Silbury still looks intact. There's not much at Lockeridge, just a rather dilapidated pictogram and a farmer's sign at the edge of a field saying 'HOAX CIRCLE - KEEP OUT'. At Alton Barnes we find the 'snail' formation everyone's been talking about - it really does seem to be the silhouette of a snail, but for some reason its symbolism seems initially disappointing; a picture as opposed to a pictogram. It's more impressive inside, though - huge in fact - and everyone we meet, including CCCS dowser Richard Andrews, is convinced of its genuineness. Apparently it formed in pouring rain. A thought occurs - snails always come out in the wet... While there, we see more parades of people with tape measures.

After a brief visit to the much wind-damaged spiral in the Alton Priors field (described as 'suspicious' in CCCS listings, but the centre was quite impressively bent at the nodes), we head for Bishops Cannings where several formations are reported to be. All we find there are the words 'THE MAIL ON SUNDAY' imprinted in wheat. The 'O' of 'ON' is reputed to be a real circle around which the newspaper's logo (for their colour supplement apparently) was trampled out. It's reasonably made, but we're sad at such a cheapening of the phenomenon.

In the evening, we bump into Debbie and Nigel again at Avebury. In an effort to find a pub that accepts dogs (after trying the *Waggon & Horses* at Beckhampton - wow, I'm really at the heart of things today; now all I need is a tape measure) we wind up at the *Black Horse Inn* at Cherhill. We're merrily involved in circle-speak when the landlord, who couldn't help overhearing our conversation, comes up to us and tells us that he had the well-known meteorologist Terence Meaden in his bar the night before, and had a heated debate over the weather-vortex theory! He then produces a bundle of photos of the Alton Barnes 1990 pictogram, the first to cause public furore - he was one of the first to enter it in pristine condition and has the pictures to prove it. He's very interested in the phenomenon and he and his wife (who saw circles in Australia in the 70s) tell us of aerial phenomena they've seen, and of how mobile telephones won't work inside the Avebury stone circle. We talk well past bar hours, but by now the Silbury Effect (ie. lack of sleep) is taking its toll, so we head back to our respective bases, noting on the way that there are no cars tonight at the hill...

THURSDAY 23 JULY

Off to Oldbury Castle at Cherhill to see the white horse and needle monument on the hill. From the ridge we spot a formation, and I'm excited to see that it's an almost exact replica of last year's Sussex dumb-bells near my home. We also see a strange rectangular area of wind damage nearby.

We get back to the car and Debbie and Nigel suddenly draw up - we've found each other again! They're very excited - there was a major UFO sighting over Warminster last night and they've taped a radio report on it. The official explanation is a laser show, but it doesn't sound very likely.

That evening, Kaye and I go walking on The Ridgeway at Hackpen Hill and find a very large field, the same crop split only by a narrow trackway - one side is completely devastated by wind, but the other, only feet away, is entirely untouched. Curiouser and curiouser.

FRIDAY 24 JULY

At breakfast, we tell the Germans about the Warminster sighting, and they seem only casually interested. As I pass the room ten minutes later, they're furiously examining a map trying to find out how to get to Warminster...

We're leaving for home today and after a fruitless morning spent searching for the Overtown Farm formations, we head down to Alton Barnes for a last look. We find a second 'snail' nearby at Stanton St Bernard! Several cars are massed by the field already. A lady from Boston, USA, tells me it's a hoax and she's possibly right - as soon as we set foot in there, the difference between this and its predecessor is obvious - the lay is a real mess, not flat anywhere; broken stalks abound. A familiar figure lounges almost contemptuously in the squashed crop - it's CCCS investigator Ralph Noyes, and with him Montague Keen. They're quite sure this is a crude copy, a "cruel joke", but they are taking samples to test anyway. John Langrish, who's produced several excellent technical diagrams of the major 1991 formations is here too and he shows us some of his sketch drawings.

But our departure can't be put off any longer. It's time to head home in earnest, pausing only at Upton Scudamore to spot a distant pictogram. Circle-spotting-wise, we haven't done as well as I'd hoped, and I'm still a little put out at Reg's prediction abilities, but the week has been a lot of fun, and it's good to be at the centre of it all, knowing that there's nowhere better placed to be if anything of note is going to occur.

An hour later, in a traffic jam at Salisbury, the memories are already fading...

Original article: SC, issue 8, August 1992

3 THE EVENING NEWS

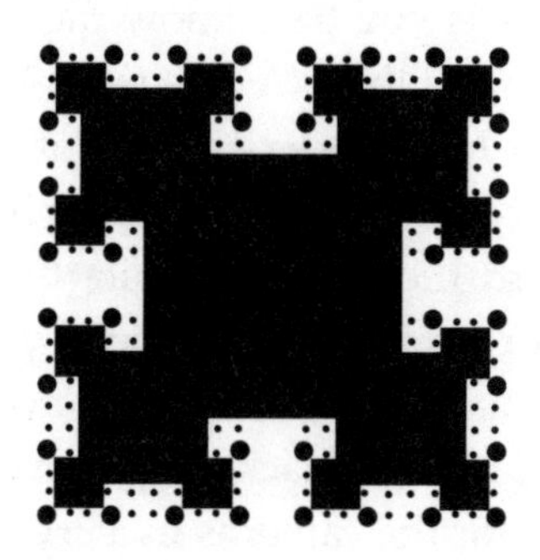

Media treatment of the crop circles is notorious for being shallow and overly-sceptical, yet there's still an odd, if trepidation-filled thrill to seeing one's favourite phenomenon suddenly thrust into people's living rooms on TV screens. What on earth must Mr and Mrs General Public make of it..?

It's ten o'clock. A muggy night. Big Ben is chiming over the airwaves. Time to take a break from watching seeds get slaughtered at Wimbledon, before settling down to football. Father lifts the newspaper and sinks behind it to find some naked breasts. Mother goes out to make some tea. Trevor MacDonald is reciting the day's gloom to himself. Killings in Rwanda, murders in Belfast. Father sniffs and turns a page. The Labour leadership contest, bombings in Turkey. Crop circles. Crop circles?

Suddenly we're transported to the skies above the fields of Wiltshire, looking down on some magnificent shapes etched into the green canvas. A voice explains for the uninitiated. We've already been tipped off by Trevor that this report will leave us to make our own minds up, so we hover in anticipation as to quite *how* a balanced view will be presented.

Familiar faces begin to appear, each with their own facet of the story. Look! - there's Reg Presley with, unusually, the most sensible line of the evening: "If somebody tells you they know the answer to this, forget it!" Look! - there's gizmo man with his 'circle tester' gadget, the principles of which no-one, including him, understands, but which apparently works anyway. Look! - there's some guy no-one's ever heard of talking about the weather and "downward thermals", despite the fact he's standing in a pictogram that couldn't possibly be explained by this outdated nonsense.

The stone circle connection is mentioned, and someone called Denis Wheatley (didn't he used to write black magic novels? Oh, a different one...) twirls his dowsing rods for the cameras in a cryptic, but visually exciting way. Then Independent Television News (ITN) gets a chance to show off its night-vision cameras, following a ridiculously huge convoy of crop watchers into the darkness, illuminated garishly green like a Gulf War bombing raid report. Glowing emerald, Una Dawood and John Wakefield give their views on Mother Earth and the UFO connection.

But now the balancing of viewpoints tips the scales the other way. Here's a farmer annoyed at the damage to his crop caused by a long line of grapeshot, trotting out the oft-repeated and presumptuous line: "If an alien's gonna come from another planet, it's not gonna land in the middle of a crop". Who says? Anyway, who's talking about landings? And here's another sadly familiar figure, as Doug Bower, who has supposedly "created hundreds of formations" (a suspect assertion accepted as fact by ITN), demonstrates yet again that he still can't make a decent circle that resembles the phenomenon we're familiar with. But it's all going horribly wrong - his claims are voiced over a picture of the beautiful Longwood Gallops 1990 pictogram. A false insinuation. The public are misled. A nation of croppies mourns. Bower pipes up with his by now very well rehearsed guff (Copyright 1991) about "his" phenomenon being "only flattened corn". "How on Earth can you fool the whole world, which we've done, with just some flattened corn?" How indeed? Perhaps because, as he has consistently failed to notice, there is far, far more to this phenomenon than just flattened corn.

But lo, wait! Here's circle researcher Colin Andrews to tip the scales back in common sense's favour and put the world to rights [*this was before he himself became more sceptical and very critical of the likes of me - such touching faith in him we had in those days!*]. He does! Hurrah! Unfortunately, someone has the bright idea of having him grovel in the crop lay facing away from the camera, as if examining stalks, and 10 million viewers are treated to a view of Colin's backside as he scrabbles on the ground. Colin, as always wearing his best suit for the occasion, bravely speaks of "extra-terrestrials" and "high nature" and of the crop circles being "well beyond hoaxers". A thousand cerealogists breathe out.

And then we're back in the air again, spiralling over a large pictogram, the voice informing us that whatever they are or are not, we should enjoy the crop circles as "landscape art". We return to the studio, with Trevor MacDonald informing us, in the surely-contractual laughing, condescending tones of all television news presenters, that his money is "on the little green men". Then it's over. The circles have been deemed newsworthy again. ITN has spoken.

The country goes back to whatever it was doing before these strange shapes and even stranger people passed across its screens. Father snorts in casual condemnation of such gullibility, mother thinks about it for a minute and then carries on with the ironing. Someone decides to have a go at making their own Bower-inspired stalk stomper. Another pathetic mess appears in a local field. Someone else is deeply inspired... they'll be out in the fields next summer, camera and tape measure in hand.

News at Ten has finished. That night, another exquisite mystery manifests in our fields, unexplained, untainted, and simply THERE.

Original article: SC, issue 31, July 1994

4 SELLING THE NEW AGE

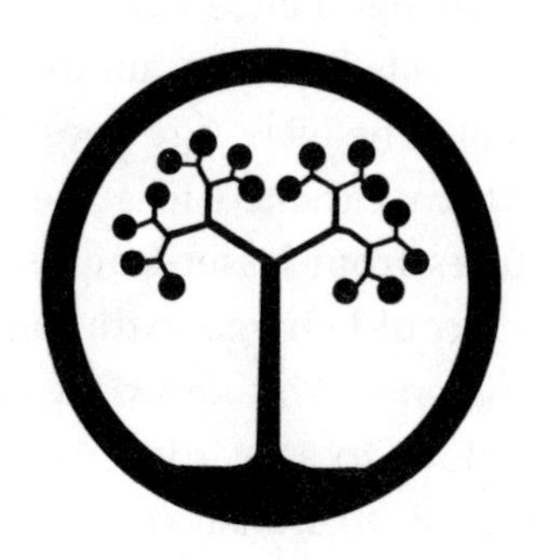

Each year, London hosts England's largest 'New Age' fair, a vast room stuffed with smells, bells, trinkets and therapies to enhance and enlighten our lives. But what does it all mean? One year I went along to discover for myself and to find out whether my humble crop circle background had really prepared me for the full New Age experience...

Many were incensed last year when the *Daily Telegraph* ran a scathing attack on the whole concept of 'New Age' thinking via a vicious review of the 1993 *Festival of Mind, Body and Spirit* in London. Were the comments justified? I decided to go along to this year's Festival at the Royal Horticultural Halls to see for myself. 'Festival' is, in fact, a rather fancy term for what is basically a trade fair, a huge marketplace where both the genuine and the bandwagonists come together to ply their wares to unsuspecting seekers.

I suppose, to its credit, little secret is made that selling is the main function of the week-long event: a place to pay extortionate amounts to find your 'chosen' crystal, sample new therapies, browse through new books to enlighten you, strain to hear yet another piece of 'soothing' music over the babble of the hall... The tinkle of gingham money pockets is what counts and no camouflage of do-gooding is seriously attempted. The deal is quite clear: they get your money, you get enlightened. Everyone happy. Mind you, a fiver has to change hands before you even get in the door. Access to certain lectures costs between another five to fifteen pounds. But as I said, that's the deal. The New Age doesn't come cheap.

Once inside, one is at least treated to a 'free' rolling programme of musical events and lectures from lesser-league speakers the organisers obviously didn't feel they could charge extra for, echoing across the hall from a stage set up at one end. You know the sort of thing: everything ranging from steel band duos to a bearded American making long, low burping noises as a pathway to transformation. Elsewhere in the hall there is equal, if unintentional, entertainment to be had spotting figures in the crowd. Marvel at the size of a certain well-known author's paunch! Gasp at the realisation that famous chill-out flautists resemble skinhead thugs! Drool at the New Age babes wandering around in force. Fall over in amusement at some of the items on sale! Banana chairs anyone?

There's certainly a wide variety of species on show here in this predominantly female gathering of both punters and exhibitors, the latter of which seem to be American in large proportions. Indeed, many of the therapies and trinkets on show seem to have US origins, but then I suppose California in particular is very much the ancestral seat of the New Age movement. Specifically, the new scramble for 'political correctness' has ensured that Native Americans seem to have become the chosen archetype to represent the feeling of imminent world change and enlightenment, going from the many paintings, representations and appropriated symbols reflecting that culture. This is a development born partly, I guess, out of the guilt-laden need to repent that western man has suddenly and rightly acquired for the historical sins committed against these people.

There's something here for everyone of all New Age persuasions - but only if Brits can put aside their innate in-bred cynicism at some of the wilder and wackier therapies and concepts being displayed. Baldness cures, burning candles you stick in your ears, oil-drenched swim-suited ladies being walked on by bare-foot masseurs, 'revitalisation' processes that seem to involve you being wrapped around something resembling Black & Decker Workmates... It's all here, in amongst the classic tarot readers, palmists, dream interpreters and the like.

A word of warning - stand still too long in any one place and you'll be accosted for sure by some bright-eyed figure in a jump-suit wanting to inflict their life-enhancing healing methods on you at eight quid a throw. My advice - keep on the move. These people are offended easily. If you refuse their offers of 'Whole-Body Revitalisation' or whatever, you are subtly but firmly ex-communicated by their manner in such a way as to leave you feeling like a not-of-the-faith outsider, a sad failed character unwilling to move forward in life by trying new exciting things - when in fact all you want to do is save a tenner.

Something else which will instantly eat a £10 note is the old favourite, the body aura photograph booth, which supposedly takes your picture in such a way as to reveal the colour of your personal auric energy fields. Never mind that this isn't proper Kirlian photography. Don't worry that no-one explains properly what the colours actually mean. The fact is that you will have your very own Polaroid shot of yourself in a haze of light. Wow. Here's another tenner-saving tip for you: 1) Take a camera and get someone to take your photograph. 2) Before winding on, open the back of your camera a crack. 3) Presto! - you have an instant picture of yourself in a glow of light. 4) Give yourself £10.

The UFO phenomenon, meanwhile, is being reconstituted by some at this event as the new religion to redeem Mankind, if some of the stalls are anything to go by, with all your favourite characters from the old religions (Jesus, assorted saints, etc.) popping up as starship commanders and alien messiahs to save the world all over again. A huge mural of an idyllic landscape with beautiful, happy people waving at flying saucers in a seemingly Jehovah's Witness-inspired style of artwork tells you all you need to know. Another exhibitor displays paintings of famous ancient sites (Stonehenge, the pyramids etc.), all of which have flying saucers hovering god-like over incredulous primitives. Clearly, some cannot conceive of these places having ever been constructed or used without extra-terrestrial intervention, which is all very well, but *every* famous monument ever?

Crop circles themselves are surprisingly unrepresented, bar the odd postcard and a dog-eared copy of *Circular Evidence* on display, although researcher Lucy Pringle was down as one of the weekend lecturers to make up for this.

Last summer, Martyn Harris of the aforementioned *Daily Telegraph* described the New Age movement (and let's face it, the *Festival of Mind, Body and Spirit* is the public face of exactly that) as "brain-rot" swimming in "a sea of muddy relativism where every religion is equal and every ideology is worth respect". But is respect for all ideologies a bad thing? The fact is that all the therapies, ideas and concepts on display in books, demonstrations and leaflets here, must somewhere have a grain of truth to them - and equally, each probably has an aspect which is wrong or misconceived. The danger lies, perhaps, in going too far down the road in one blinkered chosen direction, rather than the problem being one of respecting all viewpoints. Narcissism and navel contemplation is no good to anyone, particularly not to the 'New Age', which should be an outreach - and there is a worrying amount of this introspection on show at the Festival, which one should be cautious of.

But under it all, I *like* these people wandering around the Royal Horticultural Halls, getting off on their own chosen enlightenments. God, at least they're looking for something more in life, even if some of them do exchange one kind of materialism for another, albeit a beads, crystal and incense one. I feel more empathy for the man om-ing his baby into quietness in the lunch hall than I do for someone nagging loudly in the aisles at Safeway. And I'm more at home with these folks than I dare say I would be with a bunch of journalists from the *Daily Telegraph*. Respect for all belief systems and ideologies sounds good to me.

Some have argued that, as far as its public face goes, the problem with the New Age movement is that it needs to decide whether it truly exists as such and then define exactly what it is, especially as it's something that was never consciously created, but slowly grew up from the spliff ashes of the flower-power generation. So far it's got by without definition - but does it need to solidify a self-image, or would the very act of streamlining diversity in such a way be self-defeating, risking the creation of a new dogma?

As the old orders and belief-merchants try increasingly to stamp out what they see as the threat posed by the New Age and the increase in self-awareness and planetary conscience, perhaps at the very least the New Agers themselves need to clarify whether they are more than just a loose conglomeration of passing fads and trinket pushers. Certainly, a serious front, a forum to support and encourage the proliferation of progressive thought and inner-soul searching in this changing time - the New Age itself - is really needed right now. At the moment, the *Festival of Mind, Body and Spirit* appears too fixated on the fads and trinkets, smells and bells, but with just a little more thought and a little less emphasis on novelty, it could become a public stage for something more. The question is: what means most to the organisers - the mind, the body, the spirit - or the shekels?

I think I can guess, but I'll live in hope.

Original article: SC, issue 30, June 1994

5 DOWSING DILEMMA

The art of dowsing, in which energy fields are detected using rods and pendulums, has long been practiced as a circle investigation technique. However, placing total faith in such a method for the purposes of authentication has its pitfalls. Though internal squabbles eventually dulled its effectiveness, the Centre for Crop Circle Studies (CCCS), set up in 1990 to provide a central information pool and forum regarding the crop circles, was still, in 1995, the leading circle investigation organisation, and what it did had influence. However, in that year, a series of proposals were made for the exclusive use of dowsing as a "litmus test" in circle research, causing controversy and threatening the purity of circle reportage, as this piece records. In these days before the Internet took over as the main source of new circle information, belonging to a group such as CCCS was often the only route to know what was going on in the fields, and the threat of censorship was something to be vigorously fought...

One of the big problems crop circle researchers constantly face is the issue of authentication. How does one distinguish between a formation believed to have been made by people and one which hasn't? And with so much evidence to suggest a non-human phenomenon at work in so many cases, is there any point worrying about the man-made efforts which do appear? However, some still believe it important to know for sure, and remain caught up on the big issue of telling the difference. New ways are constantly sought to achieve this, but none save the biological analysis work has come close to any kind of fixed certainty.

The desire for authentication is noble enough if done for the right reasons, but is more dangerous if fuelled from vanity-driven worry about 'public credibility', the constant nervous concern that one might be 'caught out' by decreeing something as genuine which someone else very publicly claims as a hoax. Unfortunately, precisely such paranoia has long affected the Centre for Crop Circle Studies, and the dangers of falling deeper into it have been graphically illustrated by recent developments which could threaten the pure flow of crop circle information.

A paper, entitled *Procedures for the 1995 Season* is currently circulating amongst CCCS branch convenors and the ruling Council, drawn up without their full consultation. Eyebrow-liftingly, the document proposes the ancient art of dowsing - esoteric detection using rods and pendulums - as the only reliable test for assessing the genuineness of crop formations, and suggests that anyone, even inexperienced dowsers, should be able to carry out these tests with authority. The paper proposes that two Council-appointed dowsers decide on behalf of CCCS the authenticity of the bulk of this year's events by dowsing samples of grain from each one. If this is not possible, any representatives from local CCCS branches are expected to produce accurate results.

This could be a very dangerous situation. Whilst it has been shown on many occasions that dowsing *can* work, it cannot be used as a "litmus test" of any kind in the way proposed. As has been demonstrated on many embarrassing occasions (dowsers declaring filmed-in-the-act hoaxes as genuine on TV) dowsing is a subjective phenomenon and can be affected by the suitability of the dowser, the situation around them, the object being dowsed and the changeable nature of dowsable energy fields themselves.

The dowsing workshop at the recent *Sussex Cerealogical Bonanza* conference made a point of demonstrating how easily energy fields can be created and manipulated by expectation and deliberate action on the part of the dowser, dowsable energy lines and patterns being created and then shifted about by mind alone. The *Bonanza* dowsing competition, in which participants were invited to find, in one of four unmarked boxes, a stone found in the 1990 Alton Barnes pictogram speaks for itself - of all the known dowsers who took part, only one got the answer right, and that could be through statistical chance alone. The *Procedures* document makes the assumption that every crop circle research group has a reliable dowser who can authenticate with authority or, if one is not available, that anyone should be able to have a go and get the answers right. This is plainly not the case. Although everyone would appear to have a latent ability in the art, to be a *reliable* dowser takes many years of practice, and this is still no guarantee of infallibility.

Dowsing certainly has its place - let there be no doubt here - and could well be important to circle research, but it cannot be used as a failsafe test in the way proposed, even with experienced practitioners. Certainly this approach will not impress the scientific bodies whose attention CCCS has so far appeared to wish to attract. It is also demeaning to those researchers on the ground taking samples and actually looking at formations in detail (surely THE most important aspect of circle research?) to have circles they have diagnosed as being genuine dismissed as hoaxes by fallible dowsers who may not have even entered the design in question. Already the danger of this so-called authentication process is being felt, with one or two prominent dowsers having proclaimed most of this year's crop formations as hoaxes, despite some extraordinary and frankly inexplicable effects discovered inside. Meanwhile, other prominent dowsers have pronounced most patterns genuine...

Even if dowsing could be used as a method of reliable authentication, the procedure laid down in the CCCS document is flawed. Laying two samples from a field on a car bonnet and thinking "AURA" (the method suggested to test the changed auric field of a sample from inside the formation, compared to a sample from outside) could result in nothing more than the dowser (especially an inexperienced one for whom this protocol is presumably intended) picking up the auric field of the car or some other nearby presence. The instructional thought would need to be far more specific than this. The auric fields - if such a questionable criterion to dowse is to be employed - of the two samples could also affect each other, being in such close proximity.

With the above points to the fore, any authentication process clearly needs to be cross-referenced with other methods and considerations and cannot be accepted on its own merits alone. There is still, therefore, no way of deciding conclusively whether a crop circle is genuine or man-made through one test. If one such test had to be chosen, the nearest we probably have is the biological analysis work of W C Levengood and BLT Research, and even they might quail at describing their procedures as the ultimate "litmus test" without a full consideration of context.

Perhaps the most disturbing aspect of the *Procedures* document as it stands, however, is the proposal that any information about crop formations designated as hoaxes by the above method should be doctored to the point of non-availability. In other words, any agriglyphs one or two people 'in authority' decide are man-made, having dowsed them, would be listed internally, but no information would be made available to CCCS members or the public, and no data concerning them would be published. This is in an effort, according to the document, to stop CCCS wasting time and resources on the work of hoaxers. This position is entirely unacceptable, and surely unconstitutional within CCCS's own parameters. One of the reasons a researcher may wish to visit or obtain information about a crop circle is to determine authenticity for themselves. Details of EVERY event, however anyone may feel about it, should be made available to all. A crop formation is a crop formation, irrespective of what created it, and it should be listed as such, allowing for personal discernment. It is mystifying, in the face of all the mounting evidence, that some leading members of CCCS should still suffer such stifling paranoia, and they threaten the organisation's standing every time they insinuate that hoaxing is rife, without any proof beyond that paranoia.

CCCS members surely pay for the privilege of knowing what is going on in the fields, and it is their money that enables the organisation to exist at all. Unless trustworthy representatives of CCCS have, with their own eyes, witnessed its creation by people, *there is no such thing as a formation which can be definitively and officially "assessed" as man-made.* Such a view can never be more than an opinion, even if it is a widely held one. Information must be reported and documented EQUALLY for all circular occurrences. The document goes on to suggest that so reliable is the dowsing method of authentication that patterns from previous years should be re-assessed by dowsing the auric energies remaining in the fields. This is an absurdity for all the reasons above, not to mention the fact that CCCS has trouble dealing with the amount of new formations appearing, let alone wasting its time and efforts in fruitless and flawed investigations into the past which no-one will ever agree on so long after the event. If a past design such as the famous Barbury Castle glyph of 1991 were 'found to be a hoax' by dowsing, would it then be removed from the database?

Understandably, the *Procedures* document has come under heavy fire and it has been agreed at the most recent CCCS Council meeting that it should be redrafted immediately, although how far these measures will go remains to be seen. We are now being assured that the document was only ever intended as a proposal for discussion. However, the very act of considering such proposals in the first place is a worrying development. Even for non-CCCS members, a policy of restricted information - especially based on dowsing alone - is very damaging and could pollute an important channel of information to the outside world, hungry for circle news, with misguided and opinionated 'official' pronouncements of authenticity or otherwise, something it has so far wisely avoided for the most part. A reconsideration must indeed be given to these proposals.

No one is in any doubt as to the well-intentioned nature of the new measures. Holding together a large organisation and getting it to function well under the watchful eye of the public and the zealous gaze of sceptics eager to disrupt is no mean feat, but sometimes good intentions go astray. The eager rush for a reliable authentication process and the strong faith put into the method subsequently chosen may have resulted in a policy which, if implemented in full, could have seriously debilitating effects on the effectiveness and credibility of crop circle research.

Original article: SC, issue 42, June 1995

6 END GAME

The Centre for Crop Circle Studies' (CCCS) search for circle "litmus tests" moved on from the more esoteric pursuits of dowsing to encompass more physical methods of analysis, and in 1995 it boldly drafted in the assistance of the UK Ministry of Agriculture, Fisheries and Foods (MAFF) to perform a series of soil tests. Intriguing results were forthcoming, but even here pitfalls awaited, leading to suspicion of interference by conspiratorial forces...

Many hopes have been pinned on scientific analysis being able to provide the much-sought "litmus test" to determine 'genuine' crop formations, and one of the flagships for this, recently fanfared by CCCS, was the work of the Agricultural Development and Advisory Service (ADAS), a division of MAFF. ADAS, which can be commissioned for outside independent projects, or so it seemed, was paid by CCCS in 1995 to examine soil samples taken from several pictograms of the season. The hope was that the results might show up anomalous readings which, like Levengood's plant analysis, could point the way to providing the elusive acid test.

As the year progressed, initial results released from ADAS did indeed appear to show chemical anomalies in the soil from formations, notably an unexpected imbalance in the nitrogen/nitrate ratios. Soil outside the area of the design appeared to be unaffected. Despite disquiet from some that the results were too vague to prove anything conclusively, and that some of the sampling methods were flawed (a number of control samples were unwisely lumped together), it did at least point towards the observation that whatever process was flattening the crop appeared to produce changes in the surrounding soil. ADAS was reluctant to release exact details of what it had discovered, in the (somewhat paranoid) fear that hoaxers might start trying to replicate the effects by spraying chemicals (!). However, it did state that unusual amounts of nitrates made up most of the anomalies. Unperturbed by sceptics who claimed that a similar effect could be achieved by urinating inside crop circles, Mike Foley and David Yarham, the two ADAS officials who carried out most of the testing, were sufficiently excited to continue the work.

From the very start, however, voices of concern were raised (not least within the pages of *SC*) as to how impartial the final ADAS report could possibly be, given that government departments, however independent, are not usually quick to announce proof of the paranormal. At a questions session following a presentation, Mike Foley, speaking at the CCCS Andover Conference in 1995, was asked - by me - if there was not a risk that ADAS could be pressurised from 'higher sources' to come up with a negative result, but he was dismissive of the possibility. The fear seemed well founded to outsiders though, because of the recent 'Bodmin Beast' stories of large killer cats attacking livestock in the west country of England. ADAS was instrumental in 'scientifically' deducing that no such beast existed - despite the fact that it very obviously did, as many farmers and witnesses testified. Many of these same farmers were threatened by MAFF officials to keep quiet.

In a 1995 article, *Private Eye* magazine exposed the deliberate witholding and distortion of information regarding the existence of a wild predatory creature in the Bodmin area. Farmers reporting savaged livestock through unknown means found themselves unexpectedly being fined on counts of poor husbandry, or inexplicably investigated for possible foot-and-mouth disease cases. As a result, they learned to keep their mouths shut about the possibility of dangerous creatures being abroad in their neck of the woods, as would seem to be desirable by 'officials' for reasons of their own.

Now events have occurred which entirely vindicate those who advised caution regarding the ultimate outcome of the ADAS crop circle results.

A chain of events was set into motion in September 1995, with sudden and unexpected radio bulletins which went out across the country, stating that ADAS had come up with data which proved that not all crop circles were man-made. ADAS denies releasing this story to the media, as does CCCS, and the source of the story is not known. The reports had an immediate effect and were certainly encouraging news for circle researchers - to begin with. According to reports a person who was not amused by the story was one particular (unnamed) MP who either heard the story himself or was alerted to it by others. He immediately contacted MAFF and demanded to know why such a high-profile scientific organisation as ADAS was wasting its time on such ridiculous and obviously man-made things as crop circles. Questions regarding the status of ADAS were allegedly raised in Parliament.

Unless the following events were just unfortunate timing, the effect of this was immediate - the department of ADAS which had carried out the soil tests for CCCS was shut down and Mike Foley and David Yarham, both skilled and valued staff members, were instantly made redundant, their professional reputations undermined as a result. Most distressingly, a few weeks later, David Yarham and his family suffered a near-fatal car crash when the steering gave out on his vehicle, resulting in hospitalisation. This fed the more paranoid conspiracy theorists, though there is no evidence whatsoever that this was anything more than an unrelated accident. The practical upshot is the same, though - ADAS testing, in any useful form, is finished. Never again will official channels be trusted to perform this kind of work, openly at least.

No official final statement was ever put out with regard to the ADAS testing, not even to rubbish the previous news reports. Whether the story of the irate MP was the real reason for the shutdown is questionable, although sceptic politicians probably aren't that keen on seeing government workers investigating what they think is bunk. More likely, somebody in high authority realised that a MAFF department had committed a major faux-pas by releasing positive indications of the crop circles being a genuine phenomenon, and the source had to be quoshed at once, *very* firmly.

Once again, it would seem the frontiers of science are being very firmly held in check when it comes to researching anything which those in power would rather we didn't poke our noses into. Any further investigation into soil samples will now have to take place in the private domain.

Mulder and Scully, where are you now?

Original article: SC, issue 47, Dec 1995

7 CLOSER ENCOUNTERS

Two decades on from Close Encounters of the Third Kind, *in a culture overloaded with images of aliens and UFOs, what possible relevance could Steven Spielberg's seminal film about such things still hold for the 90s generation? Well, maybe more than one might think...*

It's dark. Reclining bodies stretch as far as the eye can see, beneath the starry sky, as if waiting for something to arrive. Suddenly something does. From the darkness in front of them, multi-coloured glowing lights burst forth in a procession, speeding towards the waiting crowds.

These are UFOs and they're being projected on a 50ft screen set up in Brighton's Preston Park for an open-air free showing of *Close Encounters of the Third Kind* to celebrate a local cinema's 85th birthday. Last night it was the other Steven Spielberg epic *Jurassic Park* being displayed, and large crowds could rightly be expected for the much newer and hugely popular dinosaur flick. But tonight, astonishingly, for an eighteen-year old movie about that hoary old subject of ETs and UFOs, Preston Park is completely packed. Not an inch of grass within sight of the screen is visible beneath the heaving mass of mainly youthful Brightonians.

Many of these people are clearly coming to this film in its full cinematic glory for the first time, too young to have seen it first time around. The reaction to it is fascinating. All around, as events progress onscreen, hushed conversations spark up amongst the huddles about the possibility that what is being portrayed might be *real*. With a Channel 4 television programme about the alleged 1947 UFO crash at Roswell imminent the next night, the subject is on everyone's lips: "Have you seen the clips of that alien being operated on they keep showing? What d'ya reckon to that then?". *The X Files* is mentioned with nearly every other breath. Cosmic conversations about life on other planets, other dimensions, ebb and flow. This stuff is clearly striking a chord with a new generation.

All of a sudden, *Close Encounters* is relevant again, ironic, given that it was probably this film above all others that laid the foundations for the alien-UFO-conspiracy revivalist genres we see all around us now in fiction - and possibly 'fact' in some cases. A question that must be asked is: without this movie, would the concept of the bald almond-eyed 'greys' be as prevalent and accepted as it is now? *Close Encounters*, and to some degrees its almost-sequel *ET - The Extra-Terrestrial*, was the biggest-ever promotion of this image around the world, and was the first movie representation of ETs as people had allegedly reported them, instead of the more fanciful portrayals audiences had been used to. The 'grey' alien beings which appear at the climax of the film clearly struck a chord with the public. But if they had been portrayed as orange blobs instead, one has to wonder whether programmes like *The X Files* and the recently-revived *The Outer Limits* would now have an abundance of orange blobs instead. And - controversially - would some of those who claim to have had alien abduction experiences be having memories of being manipulated by orange blobs instead of little grey beings, a high proportion of such cases having been linked with symbolism from the inner mind (though no less 'real' for it)..?

Given the years that have passed since Spielberg's vision of ET contact, and the now greater acceptance of the idea that aliens may be among us, the film stands up remarkably well, although it's interesting to note the increased pessimism that has since crept into the public perception of how knowledge of such contact might be kept from us. This pessimism is hinted at in both *Close Encounters* and *ET*, with faceless military squads, sinister helicopters disrupting UFO-watches, false local disaster scenarios being set up to clear areas of their population... and yet, there's something in Spielberg's approach that suggests he believes such tactics would be justified, that such necessary deception and disruption would only be for our own good in the end. (Unconfirmed legend has it that during a special screening of *ET* at the White House, President Reagan leaned forward to Spielberg and whispered "*there are only six people in the world who know how true this is*"). Despite the presence in the film of two benevolent scientists trying to persuade gung-ho military commanders that certain members of the public *should* be present at the big ET meeting which climaxes the film, that only two manage to escape detection and make it (as renegades) suggests that Spielberg feels most people aren't ready for such an experience with other-worldly beings.

Or weren't ready. Nearly two decades on, the pessimism and suspicion that something big is being kept from public awareness has grown and spread to the point where the resulting neurosis is rising to the surface in the plain paranoia and reactionary bonanzas of such mainstream television as *The X Files*. This distrust of our authorities, that they do NOT tell us everything we really need to know, has now become the norm. Although we still continue to accept them as institutions, no-one really trusts our politicians, our military commanders or captains of industry. People who believe cover-ups and coercion are for our own good are increasingly hard to find. If *Close Encounters* were made today, the lightness in tone which pervades it might now be replaced by something closer to the oppressiveness and darkness portrayed in Spielberg's own shift towards pessimistic subjects, as evidenced by *Schindlers List*.

If we take as a yardstick the many people packed into Preston Park on a cold night, and the attitudes and world-views distilled from all the overheard conversations, maybe the time is indeed coming when the public will be ready to be confronted with the official recognition that other intelligences DO exist and are HERE, NOW (that is, if they are, of course, and if people with this belief are not merely very misguided and gullible individuals...). A generation is arising which has been brought up with the concept of ETs and other dimensions simply as part of our culture, if only in fiction. If those in power and in control of information fail to recognise that these people may at last be able to withstand the hammer blow of culture-shock that an official announcement of alien contact might bring, a major opportunity will have been lost.

As the film closes, the huge mothership rises into the stars, and bodies across the field begin to disperse like ants, I reflect wryly on the much asked *"Could this be real..?"* by those in wide-eyed wonder at the prospect. And yet (though maybe an entirely different phenomenon from UFOs and ETs in the conventional sense), only two miles from this site is Patcham, site of so many crop formations in the past. Around these questioners is a entire county that has been bursting with lights in the sky, shapes in the fields, and other unexplained phenomena this very year and others past. Whole groups and organisations dedicated to the documenting of such things roam the countryside on their doorsteps. Signs and wonders from unknown sources lie under these people's very noses, yet remain too close to perceive for the majority. When the presence of these wonders is finally acknowledged, the question *"Could this be real?"* will change to *"Why weren't we told..?"*

Don't wait to be told.

Original article: SC, issue 45, September-October 1995

8 FLAKY: THE OLIVER'S CASTLE VIDEO

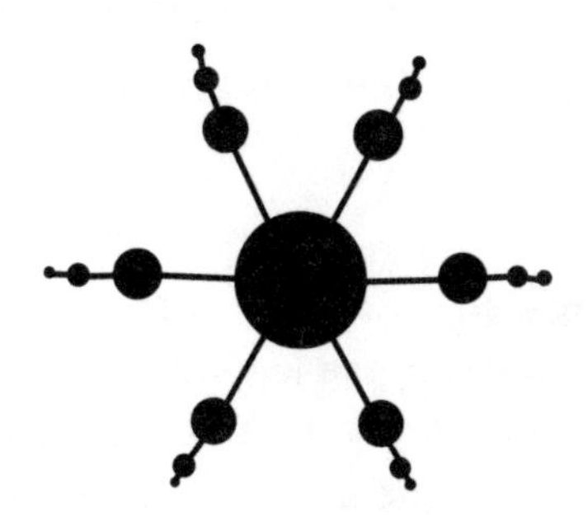

It says something about the enduring power of the 1996 video purporting to show a 'snowflake'-like crop formation appearing under balls of light that this piece will probably stir up more controversy than any other in the book, simply by daring to raise the subject publicly again. Many believe the footage to be fake. This long article remains an important document because it was written in the immediate months following the events reported and is thus a raw and very detailed account of what happened or was believed AT THE TIME - not what legend and myth has introduced through evolving retellings by various sources in the years since. Where significant developments or challenges occurred after, I have sometimes included bracketed updates, but have deliberately left it otherwise factually as was, as it remains the most detailed examination of these events, and fiddling with it could lose important little details. It is interesting to note that no aspect of this report was challenged or contradicted in the wake of its publication, even by those who subsequently chose to debunk the footage. Even today, seven years after the events, there is still fierce debate in some quarters over the whole issue, and the video's status is still not known

for sure, whatever some might claim. No final conclusions are reached here, either - the value of this piece is that it records a classic example of the way the croppie world deals with controversial issues, and of how such a seemingly simple situation can produce so many grey areas and differences of opinion...

There are some sagas in the history of crop circles that you just know are going to fall into croppie legend and folklore even as they are happening. Like all legends, the passage of time and human inability to report a simple fact correctly soon begin to blur the reality of what actually happened, and the mythical versions of events take precedence as the accepted story.

The video of the Oliver's Castle 1996 'snowflake' formation appearing in seconds under a series of floating white lights is just such an event. As with the aforementioned legends, it won't be until a year or so from now that, with the gift of hindsight, we'll be able to get a perspective on what this whole thing was actually about and some kind of consensus opinion one way or the other will have been reached by some unspoken agreement amongst the circular community [*in fact, though many plumped for the probable-hoax theory, the arguments are still going on in 2003*]. By then, however, the actual truth may well have become a hazy mix of blurred memory and anecdote. The fact is that *right now* we find ourselves bang in the middle of the furore surrounding this simple but potentially shattering piece of video. Already mythology, received wisdom and incorrect third-hand information is beginning to be stirred into the broth, so NOW is the time to try to pin down the exact sequence of events, and examine possible implications of the video, whether authentic or not, while we've still got a grip on all the reliable sources available to us. This is the purpose of the lengthy investigation which follows. Discussion of the for and against arguments which have been put forward for the authenticity of the footage are looked at in detail, and some new aspects, not revealed before, are uncovered.

So far, most of the coverage published on the Internet and elsewhere has been generally against the video being genuine, when there are actually unaired arguments to suggest otherwise, so 'Accusations', in which the sceptic view is put by the prosecution, are countered with 'Possible Explanations' from the defence. Neither mean that we endorsing the video as genuine or false. Readers must make their own minds up.

The events below have been constructed from the reports available, and from personally contacting many of the people involved. Throughout, to avoid ambiguity, names of all involved *are* included. Where accounts conflict, this is noted. We have tried to be as accurate and fair as possible.

The Beginning

On Saturday night August 10th 1996, one 'John Wheyleigh' *[spellings vary, but we'll stick with this as what we knew at the time - in any case, some think this an alias anyway - see below*] told punters at *The Barge* pub at Honeystreet, Alton Barnes, that he was going up onto Oliver's Castle (the ancient Wiltshire hillfort near Devizes) with a camcorder to look for UFOs or crop circles. At about 5. 00am on the rainy Sunday morning, Wheyleigh claims that his attention was attracted by a sound like "crickets". Directing his gaze to the apparent source of the sound, he witnessed lights moving about in the fields below him. He quickly reached for his camcorder. It would not work. Some video cameras have an automatic protection facility to stop the recording heads being used when damp is in the air. Wheyleigh claims that after a couple of attempts, the camcorder started to work and the lights reappeared in the field almost as soon as he began to film, leading to the sequence described below.

Accusation: Dew-protection facilities are very difficult to override and it is unlikely that it could have been brought to life so quickly. ***Possible Explanation:*** Dew protection is erratic and will sometimes come off with persuasion. And if the story is a fabrication, why mention such a potentially damaging detail unnecessarily?

The Video Sequence Itself

The video shows the following: first we see a long-shot of fields as seen looking south from the embankment of Oliver's Castle. The camera zooms out slightly. Then the sequence cuts to an extreme zoom-in onto one particular field. Almost as soon as this part starts, two glowing white balls of light cross rapidly from right to left and back again, turning a semi-circle as they go. Some have estimated the lights must be travelling at about 80mph and about 20 feet above the crop. As the lights cross the centre of the field, the snowflake pattern begins to appear, central circle first, then some of the outer ones. The pathways and extreme outer circles then arrive as the first two lights exit. They appear to wink out briefly as they pass under power cables or go through a hedge - this is uncertain, although some claim you can see the hedge being illuminated by the lights as they pass through it. However, power cables run across the field directly in front of the hedge in the video's field of vision and it's hard to be sure. Another light then enters from left to right. As this light crosses the centre of the field, it either splits into two or another light fades into view beneath it (this is also unclear). These lights then arc back into the frame from right to left, turn a semi-circle and exit right, one of the lights suddenly speeding away ahead of the other. There the sequence ends. The full time taken for the balls of light to pass and the formation to appear is 18 seconds. The snowflake itself arrives fully in about seven seconds.

Technical Pros and Cons

Before moving on to see how the video came to public attention, let's look at a number of accusations that have been made against the footage being genuine, on grounds which relate to the way in which it appears to have been taken. This leads some to say that the sequence is fabricated with special effects.

Accusation: The camera doesn't follow the movement of the lights, but stays central, allowing the formation to appear suspiciously centre frame.

Possible Explanation: Wheyleigh trained his camera on the field where he first saw lights. The camera appears to be on full zoom. Given how quickly the lights appeared, he might well have not had time to think actively about what he was doing and simply kept the camcorder trained where the general action was taking place - to have moved the camera to follow the lights would have risked missing something. Training a video on full zoom to track a moving object is not easy. It could simply be fortuitous that the formation appeared in full view. It does not, in any case appear exactly centre-frame as some claim.

Accusation: The image doesn't wobble as one would expect with a hand-held camera. ***Possible Explanation:*** It most certainly does! Why some have said there is no camera shake is a mystery. The image jiggles substantially at times and the camera is most certainly not on a tripod as others have suggested. If it doesn't shake quite as much as some might expect, they should remember this: a) Many cameras have a digital anti-shake facility these days, which is very effective at eliminating image wobble. That's not to say, though, that John Wheyleigh used such a device (it is not openly known what kind of camera was used). This leads to: b) Maybe those who expect more wobble aren't as good at using video cameras as Wheyleigh might be. In fact, the amount of shake on the image is one of the reasons some have suggested such a sequence would take a long time to fake - every shake of the picture (the theory running that raw footage of the field would have to be taken at some point if the sequence was to be faked) would have to be digitally accounted for when superimposing special effects of the lights and the pattern. However, some have said a static effects shot could simply have been re-filmed with a hand-held camera from a screen to add convincing shake!

Accusation: Wheyleigh doesn't sound as suitably excited on the soundtrack of the video as one might expect. ***Possible Explanation:*** The words "as one might expect" are the key here. How do any of us know how we would react in such a situation, and who are we to judge the emotions of others? The bootleg copies of the video generally available don't have a soundtrack attached, but the original video does, in which John is heard breathing in what might be an awed manner, and muttering something about wondering where the lights have gone at one point. If holding a recording video camera with a microphone, how many would start to whoop and yell if by themselves? Well, perhaps some, but just as many would simply get on with the job of recording what was going on and then collapse into vocal exhilaration afterwards. For all we know, Wheyleigh's heart may have been pumping vigorously and his legs turning to jelly. Everyone expresses things in different ways. It's also worth remembering that Wheyleigh may not have known he had captured a formation appearing - there is reason to suspect that, if the footage is genuine, he was at this time only aware of the moving lights, as we shall see.

Accusation: The shadows and light on the field and formation are wrong for the alleged time of the day. ***Possible Explanation:*** One researcher has claimed the way light and shadows falling on the edges of the circles which appear are in the incorrect places, which is more indicative of film of the already existing pattern having been taken through dark filters in mid-afternoon (to be taken away for the reverse-engineering of its 'appearance'). But we know that the formation was there by lunchtime on Sunday 11th August at least, because a number of people (see below) visited the formation at around midday. Wheyleigh was already telephoning *The Barge* at around the same time to say he had taken his video by then (admittedly the video had not actually been seen at this point). The snowflake was certainly not there the previous day to be filmed, as Michael Glickman and others had stood at the top of Oliver's Castle the evening before and the field was empty.

Accusation: There is no shadow marking the boundary of the central circle as it appears to form, appearing only at the last second. ***Possible Explanation:*** In fact, some have pointed out that there *wouldn't* be a shadow as the crops were laying down if the crop was slowly spiralling outward, because what you would be looking at would be a continuous rolling 'wave' of seed heads falling against one another, with no boundary defined until the circle reached its final chosen perimeter and the crop settled down, only then leaving a clear edge.

A Military Presence?

Despite scaremongering, there seems little strangeness to the fact that while leaving Oliver's Castle, Wheyleigh claims he saw a group of soldiers coming toward him. One of them (an "officer" according to Colin Andrews) allegedly said "Did you get what you came for?", leading some to think there was some kind of military conspiracy surrounding the appearance of the formation that night. As the Territorial Army has barracks at nearby Roundway [*now closed*] and often trains using the local landmarks, there is nothing to suggest any truth in the conspiracy idea, and their presence and the remark passed was probably coincidental.

The Video Arrives

At lunchtime on Sunday 11th August, the public telephone rang at *The Barge*. It was raining heavily outside and not many people were present. Video-maker Lee Winterston, playing on a fruit machine near the telephone, took the call. According to Winterston and most accounts, John Wheyleigh asked to speak to American croppie Peter Sorensen or Colin Andrews. However, Colin Andrews and then cohort Freddy Silva claim Wheyleigh asked to speak directly to Silva. Whatever the case, Wheyleigh was on the telephone for only about a minute and said he had videoed some strange balls of lights that morning. Note that neither here nor in the evening did he state he had filmed a formation appearing.

Wheyleigh finally turned up with the video at *The Barge* about 10. 50pm that night, when only a few people were left in the bar. In an Internet posting by Freddy Silva, he claims that the only people present that night were himself, Lee Winterston, John Huckvale, Nick Nicholson and Jane Ross. In fact one other person was present - aerial photographer Michael

Hubbard - who Silva doesn't mention [*Hubbard's presence has been reinstated in an account of this given in Silva's book* Secrets in the Fields] .

Nicholson remembers that Wheyleigh, a youngish man with shoulder-length hair and a small beard, was nervous and shy, but seemingly genuine.

Two Videos?

This is where things begin to get complicated. Wheyleigh ran his master video several times through the camera's tiny viewfinder to those present, despite telling them that this was a borrowed camera which had a habit of chewing up tapes. Most present appear to hold that the video shown that night was the same one receiving exposure now. However, Nicholson claims that the video they saw that night did NOT show the pattern appearing, and that it was already visible before the lights began. He believes more than one version of the video exists. Hubbard remembers lights being visible, but, like Nicholson, states that they seemed closer up and taken from a different angle from that of the 'standard' video. Yet Hubbard doesn't remember any formation being visible at all! [*Hubbard later cited the difficulty of viewing through a small viewfinder as the reason why he might not have seen it.*]

How can these discrepancies be explained? It has been suggested that given the dawn light of the sequence, the snowflake might not have showed up over the small viewfinder, and that the contrast of the lights might have burned out its image under those conditions. However, when researcher Barry Reynolds experimented with playing the video back through a camera viewfinder, the formation's appearance was quite obvious. Could it be that Hubbard and Nicholson simply weren't concentrating, or are there in fact two separate videos of the same event, one showing the formation appearing, another showing the lights from an angle where the snowflake can't be seen? US enthusiast Erik Beckjord has even claimed a second cameraman is visible in the standard Wheyleigh footage, further down the hill (no-one else has yet managed to spot this)! If there are two separate videos, how is it that Winterston and Silva seem to think the video shown that night *is* the same one we've all heard about? And why hasn't the second cameraman, unless he's in some peculiar conspiracy with Wheyleigh to hold back evidence that the snowflake really did appear in front of cameras, come forward? Or had Wheyleigh himself set up two cameras at different levels that night? This mystery has yet to be resolved satisfactorily.

What did Wheyleigh see?

Aside from the possibilities of there being two videos, a crucial point is that Wheyleigh never claimed he had filmed a formation appearing. But if we assume there is only one video, showing the pattern appearing, this leads to the following:

Accusation: If the footage originally showed it, why didn't Wheyleigh notice that a formation appeared under the lights at the time? ***Possible Explanation:*** The light would have been far less in reality than shown in the video sequence (video cameras are very good at compensating for low light conditions). Wheyleigh's eyes were drawn to the field by the initial lights; he put his eye to the viewfinder and started videoing. It's possible that in the low greyness of dawn, and squinting through a hand-held camcorder, he may well not have noticed what was going on beneath the lights. When the activity was over and he put down the camera, presumably he must have been aware then that a formation was present, but until his eyes had been drawn there by the lights, perhaps he couldn't be sure that it hadn't already been there in the gloom before. Presumably he eventually realised what he had actually filmed when he viewed it himself over a full monitor or it was pointed out to him by others.

The Video Reaches Colin Andrews

Very soon, researcher Colin Andrews, who has been instrumental in publicising the video, and latterly chastising Wheyleigh, became aware of the footage. In a personal communication to me, he explained how a copy of the video fell into his hands:

"When Freddy Silva met John that first evening in The Barge, *it was Freddy who suggested he should have me look at it and have it analysed. John was very keen to do this and Freddy telephoned me immediately from* The Barge *with John still in attendance. I was not able to travel from Andover. Freddy and CPR* [Circles Phenomena Research, Colin's then organisation] *United States co-ordinator Jane Ross took his telephone number and gave him mine.*

"Lee Winterston also made contact with me the following day, to tell me about the footage, saying he was going to meet John again and would inform me of the arrangements, thus allowing me to see the film. Lee had difficulty reaching him. Several days passed while I was travelling in Wales, during which time I received several telephone messages from John asking me to meet with him. He suggested the Waggon & Horses [pub at Beckhampton] *on Saturday 17th August at 2. 00pm. My aircraft departure time for the USA was the following day at 10. 00am."*

Colin, with his wife Synthia, met Wheyleigh as agreed. According to Colin, when Wheyleigh turned up he had a number of other people with him, as if there to protect him. He seemed nervous and eager to get the meeting over as soon as possible, but did hand over a copy of the videotape. He suggested that Colin could have 10% of any money produced by the showing of the footage. Colin believes the rendezvous was observed by a number of suspicious characters hanging around the pub, although he admits there is no proof this was the case. Colin continues:

"John pulled out of his pocket a hand-written contract which he had already prepared, giving me his authority to use the film in any way I wanted. He asked me to have it analysed, although this would have been my intention anyway. I did not imply it was fake and was in no position at that time to have a view one way or the other. "

The next day, Colin left England for his home in the US as planned.

Enter Sorensen

About this time, John Wheyleigh made contact with Peter Sorensen, who borrowed the master tape. He took it to Lee Winterston's video studio in Swindon where the image was examined. Winterston wanted to obtain the rights to use the video sequence in a forthcoming crop circle documentary which he had been filming throughout 1996, but was unable to obtain Wheyleigh's blessing. Sorensen, however, was given a copy and was granted permission to use the sequence in his own annual video round up of the summer's crop formations. The video, by popular demand, and in the custody of Sorensen, was subsequently shown first at Francine Blake's house in Etchilhampton, Wiltshire, and again at *The Barge*, in front of many who travelled there especially to see it. The general reaction was one of astonishment, although some were sceptical.

Disappearing Act

From the time that Colin Andrews met with him, Wheyleigh became incommunicado, his whereabouts unknown. The only contact number available for him was for a mobile telephone, which was allegedly never answered. However, no other researchers were given the chance to try to contact Wheyleigh as those with his number would not pass it on. Andrews claims he did try to contact Wheyleigh on his arrival back in the States:

"I did leave many messages on John's telephone answering service and am still doing so - none have been returned. I am not alone; others are also trying and without any luck. He made NO calls at all to my office."

The fact that Wheyleigh has seemingly gone to ground, communicating with no-one, has provided the spark for the attacks on his character, leading to claims led by Andrews and Sorensen that he is simply part of a much wider attempt to fool crop circle researchers and damage the credibility of those looking into the phenomenon.

Accusation: Wheyleigh's unreliability and unwillingness to come forward and speak openly on what he witnessed must mean he and his video are fraudulent. ***Possible Explanation***: Those who met Wheyleigh appear to have been struck by how shaken he appeared to be at what he had filmed, and by the very strong reaction shown towards his video. When he realised how important his video footage might be, perhaps he decided he wanted no more part in the process of disseminating it, scared of all the attention and wishing to keep a low profile, passing the task on to Andrews and Sorensen instead.

Private Investigations

Wheyleigh's reluctance to be contacted led Colin Andrews to make some enquiries about his background and character. The elusive video-taker claimed to be attending, or to have once attended, Nottingham Trent University. Nick Nicholson contacted the university to try to reach Wheyleigh. He was told that no-one of that name was known there.

Hiring a private detective agency (rather unwisely announced on the Internet), Andrews did manage to track down a person called John *Wabe*, who had attended the university. According to Andrews' Internet reports, this person lived at Bath, Avon, and had worked there on 'American Studies'. He now worked for a Bristol video-editing company. Calls made to the alleged home of Wabe produced only a man of "around 40 years age" claiming never to have heard of either Wabe or Wheyleigh. Because he denies knowledge of either, some are convinced this man is clearly part of some huge conspiracy! It is possible he is telling the truth and that the existence of a John Wabe at the same university is simply a red herring of coincidence. However, Andrews is convinced he is on to something here. Until the results from his investigations are released fully, judgement must be reserved [*this point was never satisfactorily settled - some time later, a television crew from Nippon TV tracked down the man they believed was Wabe, and even chased him across a car park in an attempt to interview him, but nothing was proven. An apparent 'confession' video, long rumoured to exist, has never publicly seen the light of day*].

Accusation: Because Wheyleigh hasn't come forward to clear his name in all this, he must be guilty as charged. ***Possible Explanation***: Given that it has been globally announced that private detectives are on his tail, Wheyleigh may now be running scared, increasingly reluctant to be subjected to that sort of scrutiny. Whilst odd, it is not necessarily indicative that he and others faked the video.

Distancing and Denial

After initial press releases and Internet statements sounding excited about the footage, the grey areas over Wheyleigh's identity have convinced Andrews to exercise "caution" and publicly state that the video is almost certainly fake - although there is no final technical evidence against the video itself to conclusively prove this (see below) as he himself admits.

Meanwhile, Peter Sorensen has also openly declared his belief that the video is a hoax, though he believes that it should be shared so that others can see it for themselves.

Video Analysis

Aside from all the espionage surrounding Wheyleigh, what of the video itself and the circumstances in which it was produced?

Copies of the video have now been looked at by several prominent people qualified in video-making, and, to date, all but one group have been highly impressed by the video's apparently realistic qualities. Most notably, Michael Glickman gave a copy to John Stevenson of the Jim Henson workshops, who have produced special effects for many Hollywood movies. After their team looked at the video, they stated that if faked, it must have taken sophisticated equipment, money and a lot of time to achieve. They were amazed by the sequence's authentic feel.

Steve Page of the Devon crop circle group gave a copy of the tape to professor of electronics Philip Gurr and Philip Head of Exeter University's video and television department. They were happy to go on the record to state that they would be unable to fake such a sequence even with their advanced equipment. In their opinion, only the most expensive digital editing suites, available to very few [*then*], would be capable. Their detailed analysis could show no signs that the video had been tampered with. Others have echoed these remarks.

Only Lee Winterston and John Huckvale have voiced disquiet over the footage, and they link this with a quality known as *double field intensity* and *single field intensity*. Video images are made up of two separate 'fields', and when tinkered with digitally, one will apparently give way to the other; they believe this is the case when the lights start to appear in the snowflake footage, giving them cause to suspect special effects have been applied. However, what the tell-tale signs for this are, and how they discovered them, have not been released. Until this information is made available, this remains uncertain. Winterston, while enthusiastic, believes generally that most crop formations are man-made. No others who have studied the footage from a technical point of view have yet produced the same results. A Brighton video editing company, Victoria Real, which examined the sequence and was impressed with it, has cautioned that if the video is examined on an digital editing suite, going through the sequence frame by frame will only reveal the first field anyway and that it is not possible to see the second field for comparison unless the original camera master is available. This method of observation, in its opinion, is not entirely reliable.

Nancy Talbott of the BLT Research organisation in the US has echoed this, pointing out that the only truly accurate scientific analysis that can be made on a piece of video is that drawn from looking at the original master tape from the camcorder - NOT a copy, which degrades the image substantially from an analysis point of view.

Two Scenarios

If the video sequence is a fake, the following points have yet to be satisfactorily explained. In time perhaps they will be, but at the time of writing, they remain unaddressed:

i) Wheyleigh claims he took his video at about 5. 00am. The formation was

ABOVE: Barbury Castle, 17 July 1991. The symbol that blew everyone away with its complexity. Still a favourite of many today.
Photo: Richard Wintle/Calyx Photo Services

LEFT: Alton Barnes, Wiltshire, 9 July 1992. The 'snail' - still controversial after all these years. *"For some reason its symbolism seems initially disappointing; a picture as opposed to a pictogram. It's more impressive inside, though - huge in fact - and everyone we meet... is convinced of its genuineness"* from Chapter 2, *Waiting for Reg.*
Photo: Andrew King

RIGHT: Bythorn, Cambridgeshire, 4 September 1993. This beautiful tenfold flower was the first of the true mandalas, and contained the first overt pentagram (a governing feature of crop circle geometry).
Photo: Michael & Christine Green

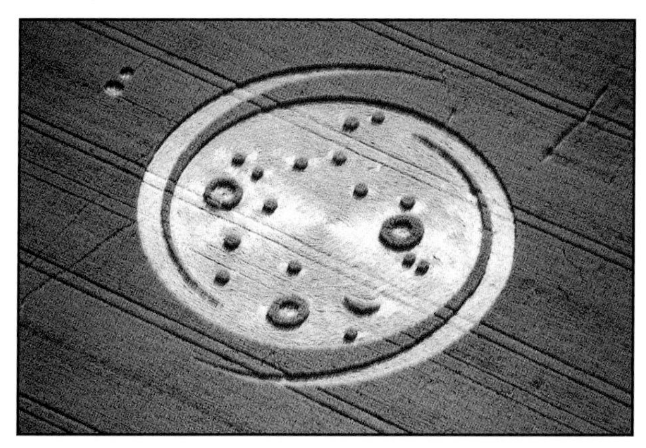

LEFT: West Stowell, Wiltshire, 23 July 1994. The best of the 'galaxy' formations. *"Astronomer Jack Sullivan... revealed that these patterns were in fact showing a very specific conjunction of planets - Mars, Saturn, Jupiter and the Moon - which would occur in the constellation Cetus at midnight GMT on 6/7th April 2000"* - from Chapter 15, *Galaxy Legacy.*
Photo: Steve Alexander

ABOVE: Windmill Hill, Wiltshire, 29 July 1996. *"An endless procession of perfect equilateral triangles, from large to small, could be drawn by overlaying geometrical shapes onto a triple-armed spiral of 194 circles covering an area of around 450 feet diameter"* - from Chapter 1, *A Concise Guide to Crop Circles.*
Photo: Andrew King

LEFT: Cissbury Ring, West Sussex, 15 July 1995. Not all the masterpieces arrive in Wiltshire!
Photo: Michael Hubbard

RIGHT: Silbury Hill, Wiltshire, 23 July 1997. One of several 'fractal' shapes from over the years. A near-identical version with a central motif would appear later. The meditating figures inside have managed to form a near perfect ring.
Photo: Patricia Murray

LEFT: Hackpen Hill, 4 July 1999. Some formations are not easy to draw, never mind etch into a field with ease.
Photo: Frank Laumen

BELOW: West Kennett, Wiltshire, 4 May 1998. The 'Beltane Wheel'. *"Visited by Channel 4 on virtually the first day of its existence, naturally keen to get a great shot from the centre of the ring, they stroll straight into the standing crop, leaving a scar to mar every photo ever taken of it"* - from Chapter 12, *Media Scrum.*
Photo: Andrew King

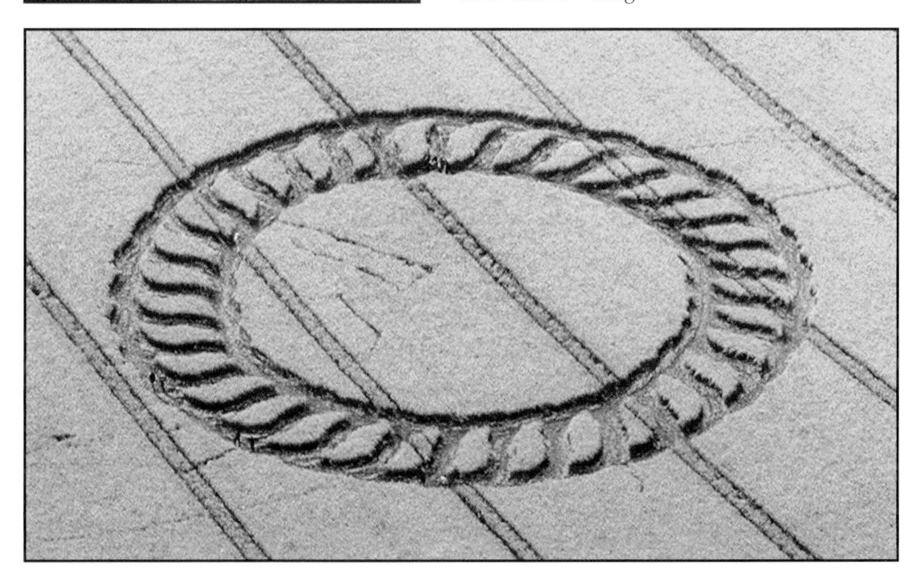

LEFT: Avebury Trusloe, Wiltshire, 22 July 2000. The striking 'magnetic fields' design, in fact a classic 'interference pattern' of intersecting lines.
Photo: Andreas Müller

BELOW: Milk Hill, 12 August 2001. *"409 small circles made up a staggering six-armed design of around 800 feet diameter"* - from Chapter 1, *A Concise Guide to Crop Circles.*
Photo: Andreas Müller

RIGHT: Crabwood, nr Sparsholt, Hampshire, 15 August 2002. *"A classic ET creature... rendered in thin scanning lines, holding out a disc of binary code"* - from Chapter 1, *A Concise Guide to Crop Circles.* The full text of the message derived from the binary code - yes, it's in English - reads: *"Beware the bearers of FALSE gifts & their BROKEN PROMISES. Much PAIN but still time. Believe* [this word is uncertain]. *There is GOOD out there. We Oppose DECEPTION. Conduit CLOSING* [a bell sound is then signified]."
Photo: Steve Alexander

certainly not there the evening before. In one scenario, he would still have needed to have filmed the pattern first if he was intending to take the video back to a studio to 'reverse-engineer' the formation's appearance and add the balls of light. First of all, he would have had to have been very, very lucky to have found the first new crop circle of the day so early to film it by chance, unless he had access to satellite photograph technology to know where to look (some have actually suggested this!). If we assume that he already had a video ready to show at 12.00pm lunchtime when he telephoned *The Barge* to see if anyone was there to see it, this would give a maximum of seven hours in which to fake the very elaborate sequence. Part of this period must be written off as travelling time. It takes 15 minutes to get off Oliver's Castle itself, and there are no known video studios nearer than Swindon, so lop off another 45 minutes and that leaves six hours in which to create from scratch such a feat of image processing. Expert opinion so far has suggested that this is an impossible time in which to do this. Even if we assume that the phone call to *The Barge* might have been a ruse and that the video wasn't ready to be shown until the evening when he finally turned up, that still only gives a day. According to the Jim Henson workshops, a Hollywood special effects company wouldn't dream of knocking up such a sequence in that time. All this suggests that the time factor alone makes fabrication a difficult task.

This hasn't, however, stopped Paul Vigay trying to emulate the sequence using his home computer set-up. He claims to have produced his own version of the film on his gear in three hours. The results are apparently convincing to some, but - with the greatest respect to his worthy experiment - were laughable when we viewed them. It is also worth noting that Paul had a template to work from and wasn't trying to create something from scratch - which is far harder.

ii) Another scenario to be considered is that the video sequence was fabricated first, by filming the empty field a few days previously, taking the raw footage back and adding on an imaginary formation and balls of light. This, however, means that the pattern would then have to be created *in reality* on the night it appeared by a crack team of hoaxers. To create this at exactly the right angle to the topography of the land and towards the camera to the one fabricated in the video (they match perfectly) would be excessively difficult. As for allegations of hoaxing, see below.

One other possibility could be considered: that balls of light really were filmed over the formation, but that Wheyleigh decided to go one better and doctor the sequence to show the pattern actually appearing.

The Formation Itself

The snowflake is not dis-similar to a formation that appeared at nearby Etchilhampton in 1993. Thus it seems to follow symbolism seen before. This aspect has been overlooked so far. A quote from Kenneth Meadows' *Shamanic Experience* (Element Books) describes snowflake symbolism as:

"... A symbol of multidimensional reality... a two-dimensional image to indicate that there is a central shaft or spindle, and an 'above' and 'below' as well as four directions of left, right, forward and behind. So it could be regarded as sky above, earth beneath, west, east, north and south".

The pattern at Oliver's Castle was approximately 390 feet in diameter and appeared in wheat.

Accusation: The Oliver's Castle formation was clearly a fake perpetrated by Wheyleigh or a team connected with him, as the lay inside was a complete mess and there were many broken stalks. ***Rebuttal:*** Simply untrue. Many who are claiming the video is fake also make the assumption that the formation is fake, without any serious grounds. Most hoax claims remain forever unsubstantiated, so this is not unusual. However, the basis for believing this pattern was man-made can be traced back to remarks which first appeared in one of Colin Andrews's Internet statements and have since been repeated elsewhere - that the floor-lay of the snowflake was messy and that the stalks were substantially smashed.

These remarks are attributed to a "CPR team". This team appears to have consisted of Freddy Silva and one unnamed individual, who entered the formation the day after its arrival. Silva, in his own later Internet posting, states:

"... The paths were cockeyed, the floor lay was a complete disaster, the walls of the circles were messy and fanned-out... This was already a mess the day after its appearance."

Freddy Silva is fully entitled to his opinion. However, one can only assume that his criterion for judging the quality of formations is quite different from that of many, as his view flies in the face of the views from others who entered the snowflake. (Silva also claims to have invented a 'litmus test' for genuine circles, which involves infra-red photography, and this also apparently proves the formation a dud. But in the absence of any data on this technique, this remains a personal litmus test for him alone.) Those who saw the snowflake on the day of its appearance, and in the days after, considered the quality to be as good as many of the other designs of 1996. I entered the formation with Michael Glickman and Patricia Murray on the following Wednesday and the condition of the lay was still impressive then. I have been surveying formations for five years [*now twelve years!*] and do not consider myself a dunce in these departments. The standing centres and pronounced swirls were quite exquisite, very reminiscent of the centres of the much-praised 'DNA' formation at Alton Barnes from June and the exquisite triple Julia Set at Windmill Hill in July. I have a set of slides taken inside showing this.

At lunchtime on the Sunday, only six hours or so after it arrived, a group comprising Terry Whitnall, John Williams, Michael Hubbard and Lee Winterston (presumably after taking the call at *The Barge*) went to see the snowflake. The weather was drizzling, with low cloud. Ironically, Terry Whitnall had also spent the previous night up on Oliver's Castle, but had the ill fortune to be sitting on the other side of the hill to John Wheyleigh, and could neither confirm nor deny his alleged sighting.

However, he knew that it had begun raining at about 4.00am, and the rain had become heavy and continued throughout the morning. As the group walked through the wet formation, they left very visible muddy footprints as they went. Michael Hubbard confirms that there were NO such footprints inside when they arrived. According to Hubbard, with the exception of Winterston, who is generally sceptical about pictograms and felt negative toward the snowflake once there, the rest of the group, who have visited many circles between them, were happy with the look of it. Whitnall and Williams took photographs inside.

When I went to visit the formation two days after, we met Peter Sorensen and two others leaving the site. I asked Peter what he thought and he replied along the lines of "Yep, it's a good one". A few weeks later, Peter had changed his mind.

The floor lay was not, then, a "complete disaster". Far from it.

Silva is correct in as much as the very outer circles of the pattern were "fanned out". These seemed to have been laid as little more than light brush-strokes, but were actually quite attractive. But this seems less indicative of hoaxing than if they were perfect grapeshot circles, which hoax claimants continually brag are easy to produce. The other circles of the formation were clear-cut and neat - so why suddenly give up at the edges?

Seen from the air, it is clear that one of the paths of the design is slightly "cockeyed", but not all of them as Silva implies. But then one of the paths of the tetrahedron from the famous 1991 Barbury Castle formation - widely accepted as genuine - is famously cockeyed, so is that therefore an obvious hoax? By studying photos of many formations from the past, we can see that the crop designs are not always perfect, and pathways are sometimes kinked or bent, but whoever said we were always dealing with perfection here?

Silva's views, to which he is perfectly entitled, have been quoted third and fourth hand by people who did not see the formation for themselves, as evidence against the snowflake being 'genuine'. But this is the opinion of one, and people who rely on the information of others to shape their own opinions should be aware that in this case there is another view to be considered. If the pattern was man-made, its quality, in this case, is not the issue on which to judge it. In any case, some believe even the universally-acknowledged very best of crop circles are hoaxes. George Wingfield, one who holds to this view, has stated that the snowflake was almost certainly created by alleged one-time hoaxer Rob Irving on the rather inconclusive evidence that Irving had been seen at *The Barge* the previous day. He believes that Irving is also involved in the supposed faking of the video, together with alleged hoaxers from the 'Team Satan' human circle-making group who George also believes had a hand in the creation of the famous 'alien autopsy' video...

The truth is that there is, as yet, no conclusive evidence to show that the snowflake was the work of human hoaxers. In any case, the assumption is being made here by the hoax theorists that the formation and the video are the work of the same conspiratorial team. No one seems to have considered that Tom Bloggs may have made the pattern and gone home, and then Joe Bloke came along by chance, filmed it and then rushed back to his elaborate studio and reverse-engineered its 'celestial' appearance.

A puzzle still being debated is that within the floor lay of the snowflake were visible but thin six inch wide underlay paths, which had clearly been put down first, as is consistent with many formations. The video shows the main pathways being created *after* the circles. However, the clarity of the video is not sharp enough to really see whether or not the underlay paths are laid first. They would be so thin that even if they did go down in front of the cameras, it's possible they simply wouldn't be visible in the footage at that distance.

A few crop stems from the snowflake were taken by persons unknown and sent for testing by biological analysis expert W C Levengood in the States, but there were too few samples and too little was known of how and exactly where they were taken for any conclusive results to be reached. It's ironic that, due to the hostility of the farmer (those who got in either trespassed or paid a hefty bribe), the snowflake was one of the least-visited Wiltshire formations of the year.

General Conclusions

A lot of paranoia is coming to the surface here. The crop circle community is presented with the video it's waited a long time to see and instead of greeting it with open arms, many have assumed it's all a big con trick to catch them out and discredit researchers. Whether the film is genuine or not, that the first conclusion jumped to is that it must be a fake, instead of saying it might be real, let's sit on the fence and see, says much about the state of crop circle research these days. The Doug and Daves of this world, who have been very few and far between when looked at in the big picture, have become a disproportionately huge threat to some people's pride and fragile belief-systems to the point where frightened researchers can't even be seen to take middle ground for fear of being caught out by those 'out to get us'. To be cautious is sensible, but the reaction to the Oliver's Castle sequence has bordered on the self-destructive from some quarters.

Part of the problem here is the murkiness surrounding the identity and whereabouts of the elusive John Wheyleigh, and this is admittedly cause for concern. But maybe he will yet come forward when he realises what people are saying about him and that his video is being shown around the world without his consent or financial gain. As well as the US *Sightings* TV show, the video has recently been shown - without Wheyleigh's permission - on a West Country regional BBC programme, and other television companies are sure to follow suit [*it has since been widely broadcast, and with no claims for copyright from anyone*]. Sooner or later, one assumes he will surface. Until he does, and becomes available for questioning about his video and alleged sighting, he will remain a figure of suspicion.

But this elusiveness does not prove the video a fake. Remember the testimony of the 'experts'. No-one has yet come up with any convincing evidence to condemn it. It is possible that Wheyleigh, perhaps being of a perverse nature, really did film such an event, but decided, perhaps in collusion with others, to use the opportunity to stir up people by refusing to co-operate in the way one would expect from someone who had taken such an important video. Certainly, one would have expected such a cameraman to have capitalised on such an event and by now be appearing on all the chat shows with a historic piece of footage. But who knows how individuals react when placed into such a position as Wheyleigh? Maybe he really is just running scared, shaken by what he saw and the zealous fervour he has seen in others' eyes when confronted with his footage.

Or... it could all be a huge, hideous fraud, perpetrated with cunning, detailed planning, circle-hoaxing expertise and access to sophisticated video technology and the know-how to use it. If so, who would want to do this? Who would want to spend the time and money to bring it about? Could it just be a bunch of cheeky pranksters or something more sinister, be it the CIA, MI5, the Illuminati or whatever?

The same questions have all been asked of the aforementioned 'alien autopsy' film, purporting to show a genuine ET body being dissected by scientists, which bears some strong parallels with this situation. It was suggested that the autopsy footage was released into the public domain to 'test the waters' of public reaction to such an event. Could this be something similar? Interestingly, that video was generally written off as a fraud, but two years down the line, evidence to finally dismiss it has not been forthcoming and some opinion is turning back to the idea that maybe there was something to it all in the first place.

Colin Andrews is convinced the whole Oliver's Castle thing is a set-up targeted at him specifically, but this assumption may be, with the greatest of respect, misplaced. That because Colin said the word "snowflake" in an interview from 1990 is unlikely proof that this is all aimed at him. If it is a set-up, one can assume its sweep is intended to be rather wider than simply reaching one man. Sorensen and Andrews may simply have been used as good starting points to get the word going round, which is exactly what has happened.

Even if the video is proved false next week, the reality is that here and now we don't have that evidence - reasons for why it must be fake haven't yet convinced. One argument, seriously put forward, that the footage shows *too much* of exactly what researchers would expect, is a strange one because it implies that when something comes along which supports the research of a decade and a half, it must be fake. Where's the logic in that? It's a good example of the negative thinking which has infected too many in the crop circle community in recent years. In any case, the video does bring surprises - many had assumed that balls of light seen during the creation of a crop pattern would be seen to move in ways which suggested the shape of the formation. That in the Wheyleigh footage they don't was a revelation to some.

But maybe, after all, it's just a little prank which got out of hand. We shall see.

What if..?

Through all the scandal and intrigue, one thing has been rather overlooked: the implications of the video if it should turn out to be real.

If genuine, what does it tell us about the nature of the balls of light and their behaviour? What does it reveal about the construction of the patterns themselves? Does the footage show anything that might give us a clue to the origin of the circles?

If this footage is what it appears to be, crop circle research has indeed taken a giant leap. More than this, it is a major step forward from a phenomenon which has seemingly taken every measure to prevent itself being caught in the act by cameras before.

There have been a number of reliable eye-witness accounts of circles forming in seconds, there have been videos of balls of lights floating around already existing formations, but never before have the circle-making forces allowed the ultimate holy grail to be achieved, perhaps until now.

There have been many attempts, of course, and it always seemed to end in frustration. *Operation Blackbird* at Bratton Castle in 1990 wound up getting fooled by hoaxers and the unfortunate arrival of a hot air balloon, allegedly mistaken for strange lights (although rumours persist to this day that real footage of a circle forming was captured - but where's the film?). Terence Meaden's surveillance experiment in 1991 had the ultimate insult of having two formations appear right next to the equipment caravans without anything being detected. The very presence of cameras seems to make the circle-making forces coy.

So if the Oliver's Castle video is genuine, this is a gift indeed from whatever is doodling in our crop fields, and a sign of things moving up a level, a hint that maybe we've learnt enough to be ready for this experience, this evidence, almost a sign of trust. In which case the generally negative reaction to the event may be a betrayal of that trust. Assuming, though, that they're not put off, this could herald further peace offerings.

Consider - here we have a video, but only one witness. Next year, bear in mind, there will almost certainly be some certain hoaxed videos going around, now that the idea has been put into people's heads, and even as we speak, home video enthusiasts are probably spending their winter trying to make the ultimate fake circle appearance [*actually, no-one ever did come up with such a video, which is telling in itself - why not, if it is so easy to fake, as the debunkers insist?*]. It'll be tough to tell the wood from the trees in a year's time. So the next step forward for the circle-making forces, to avoid the arguing we've seen over the Wheyleigh video, could be to grant more than one witness the privilege of seeing and perhaps again videoing a pictogram being created. The trouble with the eye-witnesses to these events up to now is that they always seem to be lonely voices, with no way of corroborating their stories. Perhaps this will change, and two, three or more videos of the same event, through some extraordinary circumstances, will be produced. Eventually, a mass-witnessing of a formation appearing, maybe in front of a crowd, will be the ultimate gift. Still sceptics will deny, but it would become progressively difficult for them to sustain their position in the face of such adversity.

Dreams? Perhaps. But the crop circles seem to be about broadening horizons, making people ask questions, so such speculation isn't really out of place. Maybe these things will happen quickly, or possibly it'll be another few years before the curve started with the events at Oliver's Castle is picked up again. Perhaps we have to show that we are ready for such enlightenments. It's uncertain how we're doing right now. The reflex negative reaction to even the *possibility* of the Wheyleigh video being genuine has shown cracks in what may need to be a united front before we're ready for more. We may have a way to go.

Or... the general reaction has been quite correct, Wheyleigh will be exposed as a fraud, the formation will have been proved to have been made by Rob Irving, the video shown to have been knocked up on an Amstrad home computer and all the rest of it. This article, despite its questioning, does not deny this possibility.

At the very least, the video is a fair articulation of what it *might* look like to watch a crop formation being created by non-human forces. And the thought that it might be real, to those who could bring themselves to consider it, was at least exciting while it lasted.

All of which begs the question: if this isn't the genuine article, how are we then going to react when the real thing does come along - and how are we going to recognise it?

Thanks to everyone who helped in the compiling of information for this article (directly or indirectly) and gave permission for their information to be used and their comments quoted in the original piece: Colin Andrews, Nick Nicholson, Michael Hubbard, Karen Douglas, Michael Glickman, Nigel Tomsett, Barry Reynolds, John Huckvale, John Williams and Terry Whitnall.

Original article: SC, issue 59, December 1996

9 CONFERENCE SEASON

One of the delights of the croppie world, for those willing to take the plunge, is the cluster of crop circle gatherings which take place across the summer in the UK. These provide forums to take the temperature of opinion and present new information. They are chances to see particular 'names' in the flesh, buy - or complain about - all the latest circular merchandise, and, of course, with all the inevitable gossip and scandal, commune with the eclectic characters who make the whole thing such a joy to explore. Each separate event caters for slightly different tastes and reveals much about some of the various factions within the cerealogical world. Though the Wiltshire and CCCS events referred to here have since been substantially reshaped, this piece is a valuable record of a typical mid-90s (1997) season of gatherings...

Croppies often refer to themselves as the 'crop circle community', yet much of the time seem to be at each other's throats rather than communing. But every summer sees a glut of events which does actually bring disparate elements and factions together to some degree, although increasingly some camps attend only their own functions. There are always drifters, however, happy to be at any conference or meeting which has crop circles on the agenda, whoever's going to be present.

This summer, the three big communal events were the Wiltshire Crop Circle Study Group's 'Alton Barnes Fun Weekend' on the 12th-13th July, the Centre for Crop Circle Studies' London Conference on August 30th, and The Glastonbury Symposium on August lst-3rd, which, being the longest-established event, remains the centrepiece of the croppie year for many *[this was written long before I became one of its organisers!]*

On the face of it, these three functions were so different from each other, it would be impossible to compare them fairly, yet each seemed to compliment the other, reflecting different facets of the circle phenomenon and its enthusiasts.

In truth - and I say this with affection - the Alton Barnes Fun Weekend is really a glorified jumble sale, an informal gathering with a strong emphasis on traders' tables, which allows attenders to drift in and out at any time with no obligation to do anything but chat and browse. At the very heart of crop circle country, the pleasantly musty environs of the Coronation Hall, really a prefab shack masquerading as the local community centre, recalls nostalgic visits to charity book fayres and Christmas bazaars and helps make the event the unique occasion it is. The concept of traders making capital out of the circles with trinkets and therapies can be distasteful to some, but the very presence of the people huddled around the stalls here supports their continued existence. In any case, sometimes individuals *want* to buy, say, a bottle of 'crop circle essence' (water) or rustic pottery mug with a crop design on it. Those who disapprove of such cash-ins will keep their hands in their pockets; everyone has a choice. Some merchandise certainly seems to have more integrity than others, but potential customers have their own minds and can soon suss out bandwagon tat (of which there is some) from items of genuine good intent and quality. The most roaring trade seems to be in photographs of crop formations, and the spread of these images has probably done more than anything to alert people's minds to the importance of this phenomenon. The day we start talking about a crop circle 'franchise' though, we'll be in trouble.

With all this attention on perusing the stalls, the actual presentations which occur seem rather incidental. Ironically, the talks about crop circles, shouted over the general hubbub, take place somewhat chaotically, if charmingly, at one end of the same cramped hall with the stalls, whereas non-circle subjects (shamanic drumming, healing workshops, etc.) are presented in the spacious luxury of a marquee erected outside. Shurely shome mishtake? With a few fine-tune tweaks, future weekends here will undoubtedly become a pleasant annual landmark in the croppie calendar [*indeed, the event would later evolve into a fully-fledged and well-attended conference*], helped no end by the Wiltshire group's greatest asset - the fields of circular myth and legend which lie but a few hundred feet away in all directions. Heck, the circle-making forces even delivered one of their most ambitious efforts (a 'Torus Knot') of the season up on the hill at Alton Priors for the Saturday of this year's event, which people were able to adjourn to in tea breaks. If that isn't an endorsement from the circlemakers, what is?

The Wiltshire group began life as the CCCS area branch, but, finding itself increasingly out of step with 'the management', finally declared independence. It's easy to see why the two may not have seen eye to eye when comparing the informal tone of the Fun Weekend with the traditionally rigid format of the CCCS London conference. This rigidity was illustrated neatly by the fact that what took physical centre stage at the Westminster Central Hall venue [*the CCCS conference would later relocate to Andover*] was neither the slide screen nor the speaker. Instead, the central focus was the organising 'Council' table, forcing the audience to crane their heads far left for most of the day. Such bizarre traditions are to be expected, though, and were largely undetrimental to the day's effectiveness. There's a kind of comfort in the predictable reliability and adherence to Victorian conventions of a CCCS event which is rather cozy. Everyone knows what to expect and how the format of the day will run. Their functions stand or fall by the speakers, not radical presentation, and the London conference delivered the goods accordingly, with a variety of guest speakers providing the highlights, together with home-grown London CCCS talent.

In fact, this conference was the inevitable next step from the London branch, which organises the excellent Winter Lecture Series, keeping city-bound croppies informed throughout the dark cold months. As such, this conference was less a main CCCS 'do' than a natural development of the Winter Lectures. Indeed, what constitutes main CCCS is uncertain now; short of Council members issuing the odd magazine here and there, the real work seems to be taking place out in the few active branches which remain. Maybe this is how things should be. Keeping so many contradictory theories and factions together under one umbrella was never going to be an easy task and human nature has simply taken its course, with many going their separate ways. But though the days of CCCS being a large, mothering, authoritative force are gone, instead pockets of individuals have been left to shine. The very fact that the London branch is highly unlikely ever to have any crop circles to look at [*actually, it finally got one at Kew Gardens in 2002!*] somehow seems to fire it up to be vibrant and keen in mounting the events it does, by way of compensation. Conversely, branches *with* crop circles are often the least active.

The timing of the London conference was good for two reasons. One, it ended the circle season nicely, coming at the end of another summer of wonders which could be looked back on, and two, because just one week later the whole event would have had to be cancelled as Westminster Abbey, opposite the venue, played host to the massive funeral of Britain's lost princess...

Sandwiched between these two gatherings was, of course, the annual eye of the circle season storm, The Glastonbury Symposium. The longest-running and largest of all UK croppie events, this huge coming-together of circle enthusiasts from around the world is a calm at the centre of the maelstrom, three days of reflection, exposition and stock-taking, providing a snapshot every year of where the circular mindset is at. Paradoxically, as each Symposium goes by, the crop circles themselves sometimes seem to take a back seat in favour of exploring the issues they raise and other subjects they lead into. The pictogram banners hanging from the ceiling proclaim the crop circles as the event's first focus and everything then moves outwards from there. Indeed, there's a great freedom of what it can move outwards to. Although crop circles are the springboard for many of the presentations, they are more often used as catalysts to open doors to much wider issues, rather than being the sole point of exposition. The circles, being symbols open to interpretation, renewed each year in great numbers for all to see, being so much of a mystery, being beautiful above all things, inspire so much and take us to places beyond hard technical details. It is both inevitable and desirable that their role has become that of doorways.

But the core presence of the circles at the Symposium is all-important; with the peg of the agriglyphs as a starting point, the event has a strong beating heart to fire it up, preventing the associated subjects becoming fuzzy and unsure of themselves. Maybe that's why the Glastonbury Symposium, held here annually, is the success it is; it takes place in a timeless land of legend, magic and myth, the very stuff of which crop circles are made.

This is a place where the walls of the venue are not the boundaries of the event. Between presentations, people spill casually out onto the streets into cafes and pubs, or make their way to the abbey ruins or the Tor, where the spirit of the Symposium lives on outside its obvious confines. Every other person in the town seems to be a croppie. Meanwhile, non-croppies spill casually *in*to the building to see what's going on, but because this is Glastonbury they don't find themselves out of place - most drawn to this town are explorers of some sort, happy to accept the circles as just another facet of the other worlds around us, which it is our life's purpose to discover. The event's setting in such a land of legend, the cosmopolitan air lent to the weekend by so many international attenders, and the general air of goodheartedness from all present, gives it a peerless ambience and magic which is very hard to leave at the end.

The Symposium itself is bigger than any one item on the programme.

Everyone who spoke, in the now traditional faint-inducing heat of the Assembly Rooms where the laws of physics cease to apply and fans just don't make any difference [*the event is now held in the cooler environs of Glastonbury Town Hall*], fulfilled their function well, in a good mix of styles and expressions.

"People don't give lectures - they share their consciousness." So says Symposium regular Stanley Messenger. He's right too. There seems to be a symbiotic link between the speakers who appear at the Symposium, as if an unspoken agreement has been made. A majority of the participants, without any boring repetition, often find themselves tapping into the same vein of inspiration and realisation, and there has been a developing theme over the years, namely that all matter and events are linked and that everything is not only affected by consciousness, but that everything *is* consciousness to a greater or lesser degree. The uniformity of themes is striking and hardly coincidental.

Wandering around the trading rooms and cafe, where friendships, loves - and vendettas - are born, was, as ever, as much part of the experience as hearing the lecturers, and here, sometimes, one sees one's heroes in a new light. The sight of Stanley Messenger, a philosopher of light and wisdom, making up rude limericks at a coffee table is an experience not easily forgotten. One example, written down for me on a napkin:

A croppie in Avebury Trusloe
Thought his overall potency wuz low
He thought "I should say,
It's because of my lay
Anticlockwise is crap - clockwise does go!"

Stanley admits it is not one of his best, but this was about 10.30pm. That hair can be let down in this way, though, demonstrates the spell The Glastonbury Symposium casts, where everyone is equal and no-one feels left out.

As for gatherings overall, if you haven't yet partaken of an opportunity to rub shoulders with those you may have admired or loathed from a distance and put faces to names from journals and websites to hear what they have to say and how they say it, you have missed out. To live briefly, for what may be the only opportunity of the year, in an environment where *everyone* holds what the outside world might consider weird views, and everyone shares and recognises the same reference points, is a truly liberating experience.

Some believe only the crop circles themselves matter and such gatherings as the summer swarmings described above are unhelpful distractions. I don't agree. The most extraordinary thing about the phenomenon has been its effect on people - how else can one gauge this effect but by mixing and meeting with the very individuals drawn to it? Ivory towers can be attractive places to live, but everyone needs to get out once in a while. All credit to those who organised the above events, therefore, for providing, in their own different ways, platforms for learning and openings for interaction and fellowship, of which even the conflicts that occasionally break out among the ranks play their part.

Original article: SC, issue 70, November 1997, with excerpts from other annual conference reports

10 X DOESN'T MARK THE SPOT

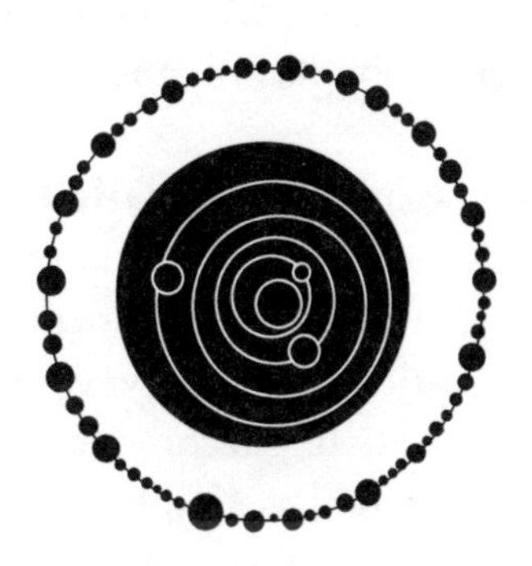

When The X Files *hit television screens with its heady brew of paranormal paranoia in the mid-1990s, it was hailed by paranoid paranormalists as the answer to all their long-unheeded cries that such subjects were never given high-profile media coverage. In the wake of its huge success, many ET and conspiracy-fixated magazines and websites were born, and public interest in the whole genre of the "weird" shot up to a level not witnessed for many years. But was the programme quite the panacea that it seemed, as this piece, written two or three seasons in, explores, or was it all in itself a conspiracy..?*

When *The X Files* first sneaked quietly into the television schedules in 1993, it seemed like a breath of fresh air for anyone with a bent toward the strange and unusual. With its fictional dream-team of two FBI agents, one male, the other female, investigating crimes of the metaphysical kind, polarised in their views yet on equal terms, it was, on the surface, a perfect balance of 90s political correctness. And yet, beneath this sheen, ran very firmly a rather less politically correct, but increasingly trendy cynicism towards those running our countries. Around every corner lurked dark revelations of official corruption and suppression.

Here, at last, was a series which championed the cause of the paranormalist, popularising subjects only previously referred to in 'crank' circles.

Thinkers of the 'new world-view' hailed it as a flagship of the movement toward freedom of information concerning other-worldly activities, clearly being instigated by authorities eager to tell all, but wishing to break the populous in gently, even stooping to criticise themselves as part of the ingratiating technique.

To the audience at large, here was simply a programme that was very good indeed, with a glossy cinematic quality unknown to most schedule fodder, and some rather original stories. Little did they suspect that they were being treated to the programme of public education that ufologists, global conspiracy theorists, ghost-hunters, psychics and croppies believed it to be.

Two years on and *The X Files* is still very good indeed as a piece of television drama, way above most of the pap produced elsewhere. But what of its supposed part in the public education programme of cosmic awareness alluded to by those most wishing it to be true? Is there really a hidden agenda to these weekly tales of weird goings-on? The answer is, possibly yes - but it may not be the agenda which many of the paranormalists have assumed.

From the very start the programme was always dark and brooding. This pessimism set it apart from the competition. Tacked-on happy endings were not the business of this show. The concepts explored within the context of *The X Files* were daring and appeared to pander to those whose views had been ignored and ridiculed for decades, most prominently UFO enthusiasts and government conspiracy theorists. Despite the presence of Agent Scully, originally posted with Agent Mulder to debunk his outlandish beliefs and bizarre methods of solving cases, viewers were left in no doubt as to the paranormal truth of the scenarios explored. We would always be witness to the events which Scully, usually looking in the wrong direction, would attempt to deflate, and thus knew the core of Mulder's beliefs to be genuine.

However, as the seasons have progressed, the darkness, which was simply an element to begin with, has become all-encompassing, both metaphorically and visually. Many of the episodes seem to have been filmed during a power cut. Even sunshine in outdoor scenes has its colours sapped by blue camera filters. The air of menace which pervaded the first season has developed into a continuous morass of doom, gloom and misery. Child murders, demonic possession, mutilating infections, bodies being minced up in chicken-grinding machines... this sort of thing has taken the place of the more varied and, relatively speaking, lighter tone of the more alien/UFO-orientated topics of yore. Dramatically speaking, it's effective. The horror content ensures that tension grips you to your seat for the full forty-five gruesome minutes. The umpteen occasions the lights inexplicably go out gives the producers a chance to use the old torch-beams-slicing-through-the-dust trick, before settling on the shock of the week. Darkness sells, and it saves on lighting costs.

But this all-pervading darkness throughout the show is beginning to look suspicious in its connection with portrayals of paranormal events. By continually associating other-worldly events and crossovers into multi-dimensional realms with negative forces and outright evil, it creates an air of repellence towards anything outside of this material reality. Thus the show no longer champions the stimulation of interest in the paranormal, but instead engenders fear of it, *discouraging* tampering with whatever opportunities might arise in real life.

When the show does return to its earlier themes, it even appears to have stepped back slightly from its apparent commitment to the idea that extra-terrestrials are among us. Recent allusions seem to point toward more earth-bound sources for those previously perceived as aliens, through some unspecified process of genetic engineering, or simply as a cover-up for some deeper government plot to abduct and experiment on its own citizens. The ET element has not been abandoned completely (this is too valuable a fictional tool to dispense with), but it is interesting to see how the writers now seem less sure of supporting this notion. In addition, there are increasing suggestions within the narrative that the government may actually be justified in covering up what it does and that Mulder may be wrong in attempting to make these things public, thus further discouraging subversiveness and consequently wagging a disapproving finger at any in the real world considering doing the same thing...

Worse, the writers have taken to toying with the expectations of the viewers in regard to the ET element, even showing contempt for their audience at times. Some prime examples: firstly, the total non-explanation for the apparent 'abduction' and disappearance of Scully for a number of episodes. We all know the real reason (actress Gillian Anderson took time out to have a baby), but we also expect at the very least some discussion of the fictional context - instead, Scully simply reappears and all is back to normal in the course of one episode with barely a question raised as to what happened to her. Allowing for the fact that this mystery will be profitable for the series to pick up at a later date [*it was - eventually - explored much further*], this is still not fair on the viewer. Another example: a girl is taken from her bedroom at night. We are even shown brief shots of 'greys' committing the abduction. Yet by the end of the story, it is proved that normal humans simply took her. The greys are a red herring for no-one else but we the viewers. This is the programme-makers playing with our expectations. Sometimes perhaps just plain incompetence is to blame. Take, for instance, an episode where animals are being abducted from their cages and reappearing several miles away, on the loose. At the beginning of the story, we witness an invisible elephant break free of the zoo on a rampage, leaving a trail of destruction. Later we see a gorilla zapped away straight up to wherever, with *no* invisible escape trail being left. No explanation is made for the elephant incident - all the characters seem to have forgotten it even happened by the end. Of course, the invisible rampage simply made for exciting television. TV writers clearly don't feel the need to justify their excesses.

One only has to look at the way paranormal enthusiasts are themselves portrayed onscreen to understand the attitude the creators of *The X Files* have towards their real-life inspiration - and thus some of their audience. Witness the 'Lone Gunmen' group, a bunch of sub-*Wayne's World* eccentrics who monitor global conspiracies and weird events, appearing now and then to help Mulder in his investigations. Although some of their beliefs are proven correct within the context of the show, they are clearly shown in a 'wacky' light throughout, not people whose opinions should generally be respected. Mulder himself, though finding them useful at times, seems to look down on them with little more than mild amusement. The Lone Gunmen portray paranormal enthusiasts as the geeks the makers clearly believe they are. These people are supposed to be the likes of *us* (ie. the sort of people who write - or read! - pieces like this). So much for championing the cause of the paranormalists.

By voicing these fears for the endangered integrity of the programme with regard to its attitude towards people with a genuine interest in the paranormal, am I simply succumbing to the kind of paranoia that the production team seem to be laughing at Lone Gunmen-types for? *The X Files* is simply a television programme, is it not? Yes indeed, according to Chris Carter, the show's creator - and this is why he will be addressing the paranormal debunking organisation CSICOP this summer. The 'Committee for the Scientific Investigation of Claims of the Paranormal' has long been involved in conducting public battles against the spread of anything that threatens the place of conventional science. Astrology, UFOs, crop circles, psychics... all are targets for CSICOP's venom - and all are the very things *The X Files* thrives on. CSICOP are suspected to have been involved in some of the major and ongoing crop circle debunking campaigns. Influential public figures like magician James Randi and astronomer Carl Sagan [*now deceased*], who recently launched his own onslaught against the circles, number among their ranks.

According to *Dreamwatch*, the UK monthly cult television magazine, Chris Carter has been invited to speak at CSICOP's 20th anniversary conference at New York State University this summer. CSICOP have been openly critical about the coverage such a popular programme has given to topics which they see as threats to the integrity of science, leading the populous into a new dark age of superstition and belief in the supernatural. Carter himself, in a number of interviews, has expressed his own scepticism towards the subjects which have become his bread and butter. Will he reassure CSICOP devotees that *The X Files* is nothing more than harmless escapist entertainment?

Anyone who still believes that the show champions the cause of new freedom of information and stimulation of open interest in previously taboo subjects may now have reason to doubt that standpoint. CSICOP and belief in the paranormal do not mix. And neither, as we should have realised, does 'the Truth' and TV schedules.

However, as time has gone on, the huge popularity of *The X Files* has ensured that any suspected subliminal agendas, if they do exist, are now well and truly buried in the intense interest in the surface details, such as the pin-up lust expressed by fans of both sexes salivating over each of the show's stars and the obsession with such major details as the size of Gillian Anderson's expanding breasts (yes boys, ladies' bosoms get *bigger* when they're pregnant). Finding a magazine right now that doesn't feature *The X Files* isn't easy.

Chris Carter has a lot to answer for. Interest in ETs, UFOs and the paranormal is at an all-time high, with many television companies and publishing houses jumping on the bandwagon, producing programmes and magazines with little or no real understanding of the true nature of the subjects they exploit for cash. Quality seems not to be an issue for these bogus journals and soundbite schedule-fillers, which simply spread and dilute the old clichés and icons on nothing more than an anorak level. One can see why CSICOP must be upset.

The X Files is still a very good show and deserves its success. But those continuing to witter on about how it is the saviour of their own cherished beliefs and a vanguard for new official openness, need to look again at the programme's development. Fear and terror of anything to do with other-worldly events have replaced excitement and fascination in the fictional context, and scepticism is openly creeping into the production team outside of it. The fear-factor, though, is perhaps the most harmful aspect, and this fear is beginning to spread through other mediums, especially Hollywood movies, which, after the niceties of *Close Encounters*, *ET* and the like, is rapidly throwing itself back into 50's-style paranoia with such films as the blockbuster *Independence Day*, a story of nasty aliens who basically blow up anything in the way of their gun-metal spaceships, while Will Smith kicks alien butt. So much for encouraging good interplanetary relations.

Some who study the possibility of forthcoming freedom of information concerning UFOs and ETs are warning that if and when an official announcement about the authenticity of alien presences on Earth is ever made, it may be based on a creed of fear - we will be encouraged to distrust and be wary of our new visitors. Recent scare articles in the *Daily Mail* by ex-MOD staff on UFOs ("a serious threat to Mankind") and crop circles appear to be evidence for this. We must be kept in our place. Authorities must retain control. And fear is the best way to achieve this, a fear that is now being spread through the likes of *The X Files*. The truth may well be out there, as each episode of our favourite paranormal programme declares, but the chances of finding it in this grim TV confection are lessening. Picking up on another recurring catchphrase from the show may be more fruitful: "Trust no-one".

Original article: SC, issue 53, June 1996

11 ATTACK OF THE RED CAPE

Sometimes commercial enterprises will go to any lengths to attract attention to themselves, even masquerading as UFO seminars to sell hi-fi... As if maintaining credibility after having gone along with such a wheeze isn't bad enough, what does one do when the BBC, in a prime-time spot, stands you next to a raving lunatic trying to contact ETs by playing a toy xylophone..?

We guess it is probably a scam from the start. Several members of Southern Circular Research receive mysterious phone calls from a PR agent trying to gather kindred souls who have experience of ETs, UFOs or crop circles. An important meeting is being set up, he assures us, to pool mental resources for a Sussex businessman interested in creating a foundation for the development of 'alien technology'.

Quite how we can be of any help with this is uncertain, but, after a bit of thought, three of us, Martin Noakes, *Nexus Magazine's* UK editor Marcus Allen and myself, as a piece of investigative journalism, decide to attend the enigmatic meeting, held at a grand-sounding venue, The Sony Centre at, er, Worthing, West Sussex.

So off we go, one sunny weekday morning. Expecting a huge towering edifice of a building with shining windows to suddenly appear before us, we quickly realise our original qualms were reliable after all. The Sony Centre is a small hi-fi shop in a side street. Resigning ourselves to humiliation, we enter. We immediately surmise that a) this is simply the launch of a new retail outlet for home entertainment hardware, and that b) its publicity machine has done an excellent job in fooling the media - and us - into thinking something amazing is going to be happening. Everyone is here - *BBC Breakfast News, Meridian ITV, Southern FM* radio and representatives from several major newspapers. The *Daily Star* has sent down one of its starlets for a photo-opportunity, dolled up in a kinky purple space cadet outfit with silver tights and wobbly antenna (ooer missus, etc.). A bizarre figure with a long cape lined in red also lurks among the battling camera crews, who are trying to find something worthwhile to film against a frustratingly uninspiring background of hi-fi.

Everyone mills around aimlessly, reduced to admiring (as would actually seem to be the point) the television sets, ghetto-blasters and sound units on display. There are no UFO videos showing, no posters or flyers suggesting this is anything to do with alien technology at all. There are more media types than there are guests like ourselves. Relieved to have some new fodder to interview, anyone entering the premises is seized on by the TV crews. We are lined up like firing squad victims and questions shot at each of us in turn. Press and radio reporters attack, clutching notepads and, appropriately, recordable Sony walkmans.

Some look disgusted that they've been duped into attending the opening of a tiny shop in an obscure coastal town, and their cynicism shows in their bored questioning. The ITV correspondent, sinisterly resembling an SS officer with dark glasses and a long coat, seems particularly disillusioned. A few are enthusiastic though, determined to glean something useful from the effort spent in getting here. Some constructive interviews are actually conducted, sensible questions asked. Perhaps the reports which materialise will bear some fruit in spreading the message that strange things are afoot in the world after all?

Worryingly, however, most of the time the crews and reporters are clustered like flies around the character in the red cape, an elderly man who calls himself 'Master of Pendulums' and claims to speak with aliens telepathically every day. This is clearly what the media wants. As we learnt long ago with circle-hoaxers Doug and Dave, sensible discussions and scientific observations can't hold a candle to the timeless appeal of geriatric eccentrics.

Finally we learn what this business about 'alien technology' is all about. The owner of the shop comes clean. Their slogan is that Sony hi-fi is so good, it must be 'alien technology' - hence the presence of people interested in the possibility of real such technology as a devilishly subtle marketing association. Marcus then makes the shrewd move, within earshot of a camera crew, of dropping a hint that microchip technology could well have been gleaned from crashed alien spaceships - and thus ensures himself a live spot on *BBC Breakfast News*. Unfortunately, this will take place, for some entirely unknown reason, in the freezing winds of the nearby Iron Age hill-fort Cissbury Ring at 8.30am the following morning. That'll teach Marcus to be clever.

The three of us retire to a coffee shop for lunch. That evening, I tune into *ITV Meridian*'s news in anticipation. Sure enough, up comes the report. It's a hatchet job, played for comedy. Our friend from the SS bases the whole report around the fact that more media people were present than ET enthusiasts, and that the whole thing was a PR scam anyway. After the briefest of interviews with the editor of *Alien Encounters* magazine, it's then straight over to the Master of Pendulums himself. With all the required 'wacky' camera angles and 'spooky' zooms, he tells the viewers how he regularly chats with ETs over breakfast, who look at his hi-fi units and laugh, saying they were this primitive once. Apparently. I sigh with relief that none of our interviews are included.

I awake at 7.00am the next morning to the radio alarm and the *Southern FM* news. Into my dulled consciousness floats the voice of... the Master of Pendulums. All that remains of over an hour's worth of interviews with a dozen or so people. How we all laugh, as do the DJs as the bulletin ends.

All will be put right on *BBC Breakfast News*, however. Surely? At about 8.45am, on comes the promised feature. It's amazingly positive. A few sensible snippets of interviews, some crop circles, Martin gets to speak, everyone looks credible. Then it's over live to Cissbury Ring. Why, is anybody's guess, as the hill-fort is never shown in its entirety and it's only very briefly mentioned that UFO and circle sightings have been made here. Still, there's Marcus... but who's that standing next to him, cape flapping in the wind? Oh God, it's the Master of Pendulums.

Marcus stands, tellingly, with his back to the Master, as if pretending not to have noticed. With trepidation, I watch as Marcus launches into his spiel about the potential of real alien technology, which may well constitute Japanese TV sets according to some. He's good, putting a fair case for ET-inspired inventions, even if Marcus is playing his usual role as Devil's advocate.

On shuffles the Master of Pendulums. Any credibility to the report dissolves instantly. The Master has a fail-safe method of communicating with ETs, he says - by playing tunes on a child's toy xylophone, duly demonstrated. My jaw drops as inanity follows inanity, all sympathies with Marcus, visibly cringing next to this spectacle. It sure as hell ain't informative, but Lordy, someone out there thinks this is good television. Never mind sensible insights, this is what the viewers want. Apparently. The curse of the geriatric eccentric remains intact. Returning to the studio, the presenter resists commenting, but his expression says it all.

We exchange commiserations over the telephone as the morning progresses, Marcus threatening to strike off the Christmas card list anyone who ever *mentions* the Master of Pendulums in his presence again. According to Martin, his father-in-law, having tuned in specially, merely observed what many will have assumed - that people into this sort of thing are really a bit mad. Martin comes up with a quaint theory. Just as the *Daily Star* hired a bit of costumed space-totty to spice up their coverage, how can we be sure someone else, thinking the event was going to be more important than it was, didn't deliberately enlist a nutty old man to deflate any potential credibility to the event? Now where have we seen that concept before?

The moral of the story: beware PR agents bearing invitations. (Actually it was all rather fun.)

Original article: SC, issue 72, January 1998

12 MEDIA SCRUM

It is a frightening thought that the majority of the world's population hear about the crop circle phenomenon only *through the very narrow filters of the media. For every good piece or programme which decides to tackle cerealogy, there are several bad ones, developed with dubious agendas for entertainment purposes alone, devised to stir journalistically interesting, but ultimately banal conflicts. The truth is usually the first casualty of this short-sighted approach, and scepticism generally reigns. This piece records the torturous media machinations of the summer of 1998, which saw a slew of attention towards the crop circles...*

We want to focus on the balls" states the English production manager for the Japanese crew from Nippon TV, sticking his head inside the door of a caravanette perilously perched on the summit of wind-swept Adams Grave, overlooking Alton Barnes. With a wave of a hand this statement scrubs the now indignant researcher Karen Douglas, having travelled sixty miles to be here on request, from the day's filming schedule. He means balls of light, of course, but inadvertently this statement neatly sums up the attitude of much of this year's media scrum surrounding the crop circles.

The Nippon venture is one of several outings this summer from a journalistic world endlessly torn between desiring to give in to the tantalising doorways into 'the paranormal' provided by the circles, and wanting to rubbish the whole thing for cheap controversy. This particular project is harmless enough; a week of monitoring the fields at Alton Barnes, a rich portal of light phenomena and materialising mandalas, in the hope of gaining the ever-elusive footage of such novelties combined. But last year the same crew were chasing hapless video editors across car parks in the hope of pinning down the alleged forger of the Oliver's Castle video (in which a formation is seen to appear), redefining in the process the word 'confession', which now appears to mean 'man running across tarmac at high velocity in an opposite direction'. A year on and the word 'alleged' still hasn't been erased from the equation. But now Nippon are trying to capture *authentic* footage of their own for comparison, the fields spread below them. A rota of refugees, largely foreign visitors, one or two of whom even speak English, plucked at random from *The Barge* pub, man the stations. Sipping tea, the ad-hoc staff glance at the monitors from time to time, fed by conventional and infra-red cameras shaking outside in the permanent gale of the Pewsey Downs. When, on one night, a helicopter is spotted chasing a glowing object across the East Field, the cameras are facing the wrong way and turn too late to capture anything.

In fairness, the shortcomings of such a hastily-arranged watch (devised only a couple of weeks before) are recognised by the largely benevolent Nippon crew, and a far more organised assault is planned for 1999. All of this enterprise shows far more imagination than some of the other media circle exercises carried out this summer. TV crews have been lurking out there in the fields since the very beginning of this season. In a portent which, looking back, was a symbol of things to come, the April 'Beltane Wheel' formation at West Kennett Long Barrow managed to get visited by Channel 4 on virtually the first day of its existence. Naturally keen to get a great shot from the centre of the ring, they strolled straight into the standing crop, leaving a scar to mar every photo ever taken of it - and this just to film a link for a science fiction season in which a space-suited figure wanders the formation (turned blue by video effects). As a metaphor for walking all over the crop circle phenomenon this is pretty good.

Fast-forward to the Alton Barnes circle celebration weekend of July (which also attracts local TV coverage) and we find a national TV crew out to do just that. Uninvited, they turn up and pin people against walls, firing questions about why they believe the circles are a genuine phenomenon and how they feel about hoaxing. Finally, helpers from the Wiltshire group in turn manage to pin *them* down and organise the situation slightly. Official permission to film is given. It's the BBC, making a report on crop circles for BBC 2's *Country File*. Faint alarm bells ring. Weren't these the people who had Doug Bower try (unsuccessfully) to fool Lucy Pringle with a hoaxed pattern the year before? But surely they wouldn't cover the same ground again? The crew proceed to film freely and decide to record my own presentation. As I speak, the camera pops up in unexpected places around the stage, at one point appearing behind me, peering at the amused audience from between my legs... more focusing on the balls? All seems well until one of the crew lets slip that our old friend Bower, together with those other ubiquitous 'landscape artists', operating under the laughably puerile moniker 'Team Satan', will be creating formations for their cameras in the area the following weekend. It transpires later that the whole designated slot of the programme, to be shown in January 1999, is to be devoted largely to the hoax phenomenon and the lives of these marvellous people who supposedly brighten up the countryside with their creations each summer. [*Indeed, the final ghastly product was a ridiculous hymn to the talents of Doug Bower and those inspired by him, blah blah, with barely a trace of balancing viewpoints from the other side.*]

A week later, and these artists aren't too hard to find. Tipped off, a group waiting up on Knap Hill soon spot the glow from... the floodlights. As ever, these "Made at night, folks" designs need the aid of lots of electricity. Interlopers find their way to the field in question and begin to harangue the crop-squashers inside with taunts, to the degree that at one point Bower is forced to retreat to the safety of his car. Those trying to enter the fields are firmly repelled by the TV crew, armed with arc lights, cranes and cameras. In a surreal twist, threats are made that the police will be called to remove the *observers*, so that the 'artists' may continue their work...

A few weeks later still, and the police reputedly have to mount an overnight watch on a formation made by the same team for Mitsubishi, a picture of a car, carved with two days of great effort into the East Field (a month before, BT have the numbers '03' created at Oliver's Castle for a code number ad). The guard is there with good reason. Vigilante croppies have been threatening to trounce the creation as some kind of poetic justice, and the advertisers, paying good money for the services of Team Satan, not to mention the permission of the farmer, are taking no chances. They still want it there the next day so it can be photographed and videoed for their advertising campaign. Amusingly, belching 'smoke' does somehow get added to the exhaust pipe a few days later - not a good advert for catalytic converters.

But the world of television isn't done with the circles yet. I'm invited onto ITV's breakfast show *GMTV*. Do I know of any formations they can go and film? I help them with names and numbers. Then I learn they have no intention of viewing any new patterns at all - apart from one. 'Former circlemaker' (as the show describes him) Rob Irving has been commissioned, in an astonishingly imaginative move, to make a crop formation for the cameras instead. As I'm chauffeur-driven up to the London studios, drizzle spattering the windscreen, I reflect comfortingly on the fact that I will be cozy 'on the sofa' with the presenters while Rob sweats it out in a damp, blustery field. The slot begins. We watch his creation being made on the monitors. We are shown highlights of the three hours it takes to make a pretty small (and pretty rough inside) nest of crescents. At a safe distance of about two hundred miles, Irving and I exchange our views, live, to a few million viewers. The mood is surprisingly convivial (Irving: "Hi, Andy"). And then we go home again. One rather more innocuous television adventure is mounted: the cable channel *L!ve TV* spend a day taking footage of circles and researchers for their programme *The Why Files*. For once, the presenter (and writer) is genuinely positive about crop circles - as he was when they covered the phenomenon in 1996. The final result promises to be a good experience. In an ultimate irony, faulty sound equipment later leads to much of the footage having to be junked (including all of my own), the sequences finally shown being much curtailed from that planned...

So much for television ventures. What about the newspapers this summer? Each season, two or three papers usually wind up featuring the circles in a quiet week. This year, *The Independent* runs a colour spread of photos and a fairly innocent piece (for the press anyway), the *News of the World* includes the phenomenon as part of their travel section, recommending them as reasons to travel to Wiltshire, and the Alton Barnes weekend conference sparks a few mentions. *Fortean Times* and *Tomorrow's World* magazine sneer with sceptic propaganda as we expect. And then there is the article in *The Guardian*.

A high-profile journalist for the paper telephones a number of croppies early in the season, including myself, promising an incisive and open piece about crop circles, which will be pleasant and non-judgemental. He begs me for a proof copy of my forthcoming book *Vital Signs* (not then published) for research purposes. To each person he speaks to, promises are made of what the pieces will be, of how positive a light croppies will be painted in, of what he will and won't be doing. In short, he tells each what they want to hear in order to obtain the information he needs.

He attends the Alton Barnes weekend and immediately there are warning signs. In fact, I have already had a portent of what is to come by the fact he has recently asked me about the telephone numbers of well-known 'hoaxers', who at that point he has not spoken to. In the final piece he claims he made no attempt to contact hoaxers - they approached him. Not true. Or at least, if they got to him first, he certainly had every intention of reaching them anyway. At the Alton Barnes do, the journalist's behaviour towards me is odd to say the least. Having never met the man in person, I don't recognise him when he speaks to me and attempts to ask me questions. He knows who I am, but never introduces himself by name, his body language cold and hostile. As a result of this and the inconvenient moments he chooses to approach me, we never do speak for any length of time. Only later do I discover his identity. Yet this is a man I have had lengthy conversations with on the telephone in the weeks prior. Why not introduce himself? It's as if he wants information from me, but wants to keep his distance, not wanting to give too much away. Later, at the closing ceremony of the weekend, conducted by Native American Rod Bearcloud in the East Field mandala, the journalist huddles outside the circle of hand-linked figures with the 'hoaxers' who have strolled openly around the event all weekend. He disappears with them to *The Barge*.

Unsurprisingly, when the long piece in *The Guardian* materialises a week or two later in its colour supplement, it is the usual hymn to the sincerity and talent of the human circlemakers we have come to expect from the media, at the expense of exploring the true history and details of a phenomenon which simply cannot be explained in these terms alone. Worse, the journalist has openly colluded with the hoaxers and claims to have attended the creation of a mandala which arrived near Silbury Hill in July (created, if the claim is true, as a criminal act, as no permission was sought from the farmer). There's some attempt to balance the arguments over the circles' origins, but by and large croppies are portrayed as loveable but rather stupid eccentrics, blind to truth, heads firmly up their own behinds. The usual ludicrous hoaxing claims are repeated and left unchallenged. Few of the opposing facts and figures given by those researchers who helped the journalist are included. The reams of scientific evidence specifically sent from W C Levengood's laboratories in the US aren't even mentioned. I am not credited, nor *Vital Signs* referenced, despite clearly being a major aid to background information. An air of betrayal pervades a largely philosophical piece on the nature of belief and human ingenuity, in which the facts are deemed irrelevant.

The basic thread of the article can be gauged by perusing the following excerpt from a letter sent by researcher Michael Glickman (heartwarmingly referred to in the piece as a "cadaverous old man") to the journalist in its wake:

It has taken me almost a week to reach a state of calm sufficient to write to you. Your article was a travesty and a betrayal of our implicit understanding. Above all, it was a shoddy piece of journalism which repeats the same old tired and dishonest story and does a gross disservice both to your readers and your own reputation.

Let me start with shoddy journalism and a list of errors which might easily have been checked.

Bearcloud is a member of the Osage tribe not the "Odege". Rod Bearcloud himself is from Arizona, but the Osage is an Oklahoma tribe.

The widespread use of the word 'believer', both in and out of quotes, reveals just how close you were to the hoax claimants. This is - as you clearly know - a demeaning word used by them to refer to crop circle researchers. It is rarely used in the community.

Francine Blake's magazine is The Spiral, *not* The Sphere. *The Doug and Dave scam started in 1991 not 1992. They were not artists, though one of them was a picture framer. Incidentally, though they made many claims and performed often for the cameras, there is no solid evidence that they carried out a single hoax as such.*

Why are there quotation marks around "sacred" in sacred geometry? What kind of "journalism" is this? Julian Richardson, not Richards. Rob lrving not Ian Irving. Fibonacci not Fibbanucci.

When you first called me, I expressed my reservations. I have long and bitter experience of media trivialisation of what might be the most important events on earth, and I made it clear that I would not participate in another hoax-boosting exercise. You assured me that you wanted to do a serious article. You were certain that something strange was happening and you felt it important - at last - to deal with this at a more thorough level.

I knew and admired your work... and so I trusted you. My colleagues warned me that I was to be duped, but I went out of my way to speak of your integrity and good intentions. Because of my faith in you, many of them went along with this enterprise.

You spent four hours here talking to me, you called me at least six further times for information and contacts, and my assistant Debbi Sprinkle took you into a formation.

It soon became clear which way things were to go. You spent more and more time with the claimants and, as the article showed, you were conned, as were we, as were your readers.

They call themselves "pranksters", but they are conmen. And when did you hear of a conman who was not plausible?

I am affronted by the way words were put into my mouth. I am shocked by the tongue-in-cheek treatment of Stanley Messenger and Rod Bearcloud, both - whatever else their views - of radiant integrity. Easy shots at soft targets.

Above all, I find it a disgrace that The Guardian's *position has sunk so low that it has become an unquestioning mouthpiece for known liars.*

What is it about the media that those who work within it cannot find it in themselves to see beyond the myths spread by those who seem to delight in keeping the true scale and background of the crop circles quiet, and instead pushing alleged landscape artists to the fore as those responsible for the whole thing?

The truth is that everyone wants quick-fix answers to a phenomenon which just cannot be explained in simple terms. The answer, if any is ever forthcoming, may be far more sophisticated than the question, residing on a level far deeper than the questioners will ever understand. But try telling that to a reporter. The many facets to the mystery, the associated strange phenomena, the scientific and statistical evidence, the fine detail of the ways the circles appear to be created - it's all too much to be absorbed in the two or three weeks a representative from the media may spend (if that) researching any piece. How can they possibly absorb or understand in such a tiny period what some in the circle community have spent years accumulating and trying to come to terms with, piece by piece? And yet, arrogantly, into the circle world they walk for the briefest of moments, and out again, believing they have sussed everything there is to know, with some kind of incredible outside wisdom which mysteriously eludes those with long-time personal experience.

The media doesn't like mysteries. It prefers to deal in absolutes. If it doesn't find them it will invent them, and human artistry is easy to latch on to as the quick-fix solution. Occam's Razor is relentlessly slashed at anything which even hints at mystery, and grey areas aren't allowed. The media doesn't like beauty, it likes controversy. Where there is no controversy, it will stir it up and salaciously report the resultant action, hence the endless provocative setting up of hoaxers against 'believers'. It doesn't want to hear about the effect the splendour of the circles is having, it wants arguments, discussion, fire and ridicule, something to entertain the readers or viewers. We should no longer expect anything else. The American linguistics professor Noam Chomsky has devoted an entire life to exposing the manipulative narrow-mindedness of the media. Not surprisingly, though grudgingly respected, outside of intellectual circles he remains a fringe figure as far as the general public are concerned. Where Chomsky's words fall on deaf ears, why should we hope for more?

So much for the journalism. What of the stooges themselves who are endlessly encouraged by the media, the guerrilla artists we are supposed to believe in? What have we learnt about them this summer? The US TV venture in New Zealand earlier in the year had already shown us that Team Satan could make reasonable facsimiles of what appears in the fields every night of every summer, but that the time they took to make their demonstration and the shortcomings contained within severely challenged the notion of the mass-hoaxing scenario explaining more than a proportion of the crop formations. Yet for some casual and uninformed observers, the mystery was solved as far as they were concerned. Given this, what was left to prove by making yet another demonstration? Yet in comes the BBC, itself for the second year running, and commissions another. Like the New Zealand formation before it, its intent was ingenious - a pattern impressive to the eye, lots of circles in a striking motif, but geometrically naive and straightforward to make. Why waste time even trying to attempt some of the sublime geometrical qualities seen in many crop glyphs when you know large sections of the public will be fooled by pretty, but basic stuff?

With straightforward and typically uncomplicated lays, the Team Satan designs were at least far better than the messy floor left by Doug Bower's traditionally shoddy efforts further up the same field (a copy of the quartered Winterbourne Stoke circle of 1989, with large grapeshot), even if the shapes of the circles themselves were good. Again, the man-hours needed to create these relatively modest-sized patterns, as with the roughly-laid Mitsubishi car, which took two days to create, show the long time that would be required to make some of the larger, more complex designs seen over the years. The small nest of crescents for *GMTV* took two people (Irving and a presenter) three hours to lay and was unimpressive on the ground, as the cameras all-too-plainly revealed. And still no-one has ever attempted to recreate the subtle spiral sweeps and huge ambition of formations like the Windmill Hill fractal of 1996, 194 circles in triple arms spanning something like 600 feet. Maybe eventually, one of these alleged artists will work out a method and make an attempt, but who will believe them after several years in which to learn and prepare? Why couldn't they recreate such skills when first asked?

Those who claim to be out there creating the phenomenon we know and love have uncomfortably exposed themselves this year in a number of ways. Their former stated position, that to reveal their methods would compromise their status as true artists, has been well and truly thrown out the window. Money and fame has beckoned and any such principles are long gone. It also begs the question of why people such as Team Satan should bother heading out from London (their home) each night of every summer to sweat out fruitless hours of effort in making crop circles for no reward and no recognition when they can be openly paid and commissioned to do so instead, endlessly fuelled by small-minded TV companies and pony-tailed ad execs thinking they've come up with an original concept. As far as anyone knows, these publicity stunts may well be their entire sum total efforts for the year. It's something that may be put to the test: man-made methods and styles have been revealed for all to see now and will be looked for with greater scrutiny in future patterns by those obsessed with sorting (literally) wheat from chaff.

And where are all the other hoaxing teams sceptics would have us believe exist? Seeing the lucrative gravy train the 'outed' artists seem to be riding, is it unreasonable to suppose they might also have come forward to grab a piece of the action by now? Yet, after all this time, only a handful of 'circlemaking' individuals are known of, ones who couldn't account for more than a proportion of each summer's formations.

There's little to show the claimants are really interested in art for art's sake when it comes to the circles. It's the attraction of artifice which seems to drive them on, of creating that which fools the eye, which purports to be something it isn't. They've learnt their craft well. They and the few other operators have discovered how to squash crop as well as people will ever squash crop. Those who choose to deny their handiwork - some still refuse to accept that some of the demonstration formations of this year were man-made, despite ground evidence in one case and eye-witnesses and film of the circles being made in the other! - aren't being quite fair and shouldn't be afraid to attribute a human source to a few designs. But the human circlemakers' work remains a pale shadow of the masterpieces we have seen, and the source of their inspiration remains something which long predates their plagiarism and strongly suggests far less mundane origins. Yet still the old tired mass-hoaxing myths are trotted out, even by those who really should know better by now.

A ludicrous Centre for Crop Circle Studies 'study paper' about hoaxing, recently circulated amongst Council members, demonstrated how short a distance some have come over the years: seven pages of long out-of-date hypothesis (masquerading as fact) about alleged circlemaking groups like the 'Wessex Sceptics', who haven't shown the remotest interest in the circles for years, yet are here promoted as the masterminds behind a huge global conspiracy to discredit the phenomenon, backed by a shadowy Masonic 'Illuminati'. There *is* a little evidence to show there may have been a coordinated campaign of disinformation against the crop circles, for sure, but the unproven assumptions and misperceptions about the levels of hoaxing and how to detect it (based mostly on flawed photo observation), as contained in this document, are breathtakingly naive. Such discussion papers do nothing but play into the egos of the few human circlemakers there are, whose intentions and aims, for the most part, appear to be far less highbrow and organised. This type of scaremongering document (which, incidentally, suggests farmers are 'in' and involved with the whole hoax thing..!) simply focuses unnecessary attention onto the hoaxers and will do nothing but spread yet more unfounded uncertainty.

None of what human circle-making activity there is, often stirred up by a narrow-minded media, has proved anything beyond what we already knew about these people's abilities or lack of them. And, frankly, no demonstration or supposed big 'expose' (paranoiacally feared in the CCCS study paper) ever will. The public can be fooled by almost anything, because they're kept in ignorance of balancing factors most of the time (*The Guardian's* deliberate omissions demonstrate this all too well), but for those already convinced of the phenomenon's veracity, too many chances have been passed up by the claimants to show they can match the best formations, and most of the big questions remain unanswered. The stalemate will continue, and whatever section of the public may fall away through shallow trust in the words of the media, the mystery will survive for those with eyes to see.

One almost feels sorry for the journalists trapped in their own narrow worlds and the hired hands who make their circles for them. At the closing ceremony of the Alton Barnes weekend, a ring of over a hundred people stand, hands linked, watching Rod Bearcloud perform his rather beautiful ritual and haunting chant. A bit New Age for some, perhaps. An easy target for cynicism. Yet beautiful for all that. But who are these strange people who hover just outside the ring of flesh and blood? A selection of the alleged human circlemakers huddle uneasily at the edges of the seven-fold mandala, while *The Guardian* journalist prowls, camera in hand (the ring of people will be the visual centrepiece of the article). It's as if they desperately want to be part of it all, but are held back, frustratingly contained by their self-proclaimed status, unable to join in, but unable to keep away.

"They need us and we need them" says Rob Irving on *GMTV*, or words to that effect. There are few croppies who could honestly say they needed the likes of the circle claimants in return, but in one respect his words touch on a key point. He and his kin *do* need us, because without 'the believers' there's no fuel for their ambition, whatever the motives may be - but if they all stopped their alleged antics tomorrow, the strong chances are we would still have a phenomenon, a view the evidence supports, both scientific, geometric, statistical and 'paranormal'. A delusional and ludicrously blind view, the sceptics will shout. I am specifically described in the recent CCCS document (nonsensically citing *Vital Signs*, a book that could not possibly have been read when this paper was written) as one who will suffer 'serious psychological problems' when the true scale of hoaxing is revealed. I won't be reaching for the Prozac just yet.

But then, as they keep telling me, in the words of the old song, I'm a believer.

Original article: SC, issue 80, September-October 1998

13 THE WORLD IS FULL OF MARREE MAN

When the largest representation of a human figure in the whole of history was found etched into an Australian desert in 1998, it stimulated little more than a few column inches in the world's press, but did initiate a mysterious treasure hunt on the other side of the world. Yet, the huge aboriginal-looking man still remains totally unexplained...

In August 1990, in the very weeks of the first extraordinary summer of English pictogram crop formations, a huge 'sriyantra' - a kind of complex Indian mandala - was found etched into a dry lake bed at Mickey Basin in Oregon. Its dimensions were immense (about a mile across) and its accuracy astonishing. The thin lines making up the pattern totalled 13.3 miles in length... No vehicle tracks or other obvious signs of human activity were visible. After a big fuss in the local US media, in a Doug and Dave-type scenario depressingly familiar to crop circle aficionados, a local 'artist' and his mates eventually laid claim to it.

The demonstration 'art' they then made using a mechanical cultivator was shockingly crude and bore no resemblance whatsoever to the quality or scale of the original sriyantra, but the media accepted their story anyway and so the mystery was conveniently buried in the time-honoured fashion.

In the summer of 1998, a similar situation presented itself in southern Australia. In an unfolding saga which was only sporadically reported in the media, a colossal 4km-long figure of a naked Aboriginal human figure, apparently poised as if to throw some type of stick, was discovered ploughed into a plateau in the desert 600km north of Adelaide. The design was fluid, accomplished and rather beautiful. Each line which made up the pattern was around 90 feet wide and the total circumference of the figure was a staggering 28km..! Whatever or whoever made it wasn't just mucking about. Indeed, it has been claimed as the largest single piece of art ever found.

Named 'Marree Man' after the local area, the accusations began to fly pretty quickly. Chris Headley, an Australian artist who has created several pieces of land art, was first suspected of authorship, but denied it, pointing out, pertinently, that the largest design he had ever made was just 300m across - and he was impressed. The military - that old fallback - then became the focus, after reports of Australian army vehicles seen manoeuvring in the area, although some believe they were investigating the mysterious appearance. The US military also fell under scrutiny as American servicemen stationed at Woomera had apparently been considering the preparation of a commemorative desert etching before pulling their forces out within the next two years, but again there was a categorical denial (for what that's worth from the military). In time, everyone from Aboriginal protesters to workers from the Western Mining Corporation (also in the area) became suspects, with little evidence in any direction.

Incredibly - or perhaps deliberately - with all the accusations flying, barely anyone stopped to consider how Marree Man might have been created. Such a feat would be a Herculean task and on such a scale would almost certainly require serious surveying techniques and satellite-linked global positioning systems to ensure the accuracy displayed. Close-up photos showed each line was made up of a number of strips, suggesting some kind of ploughing instrument could have been pulled in successive relays, but to know just where to manoeuvre to such a detailed degree, when on that scale any element of the design would be completely indiscernible on the ground, would be a major challenge to say the least.

At last, as if to fill the uncomfortable vacuum of uncertainty surrounding the whole business, an easy answer came and allowed everyone to relax into disinterested ignorance again. A series of cryptic faxes began to be sent to the Australian media, giving mysterious and elusive clues to a claimed purpose for Marree Man, though its physical origins were not explained. And then the mystery touched our shores with the arrival of similar faxes to pubs and hotels surrounding the famous chalk hill figures of England. First, the village of Cerne Abbas, Dorset, home to the beclubbed and rather well-endowed 'giant', was contacted, and then, closer to my home (and a well-known crop circle site), hoteliers around the 'Long Man of Wilmington', a figure apparently clutching two staves, received instructions directing them to a site near the Long Man himself. Local newspapers and TV crews had already been alerted and were waiting for them. Digging unearthed a container with three laminated cards within, giving clues as to the whys of Marree Man, but again no reference to the hows. On the cards were the following:

"The Maala Hunt [their apparent name for Marree Man] *and the concept of a large-scale mystery were created for two reasons only: as a potentially permanent benefit to the state of South Australia through increased tourism and international profile, and also to honor the proud way of life and inherently athletic pursuits of the indigenous people for the Sydney Olympiad."*

And so Marree Man - the largest representation of a human being found in history - was written off as a cheap advert for Australian tourism and a plug for the forthcoming Sydney Olympics. This, like Doug and

Dave's circular exploits and the Oregon sriyantra claims, was accepted widely without a single shred of evidence nor a rational explanation of how it might have been achieved. The faxes' unknown authors only *imply* creatorship of the figure, but most seemed happy not to question further. The faxes worked perfectly as a trivial distraction from other issues and stranger potential explanations, and the media appeared eager to sweep the whole matter under the carpet. Early reports that used toilet paper was found in the area soon after were enough for some to dismiss it (find a 4km square area of countryside that doesn't have loo paper, a discarded tampon or used condom somewhere and you'll be doing well). Some Australians condemned the figure as crass "vandalism", and even local Aboriginal tribes, who one might have thought would feel complimented, branded it "offensive", considering it an inflammatory intervention (from whoever) into local ongoing tribal land rights disagreements.

There well may be a mundane explanation for Marree Man's appearance, but as yet there is no solid evidence for one, despite a general acceptance of the 'tourist advert' theory. This has not been aided by a dearth of direct research information available for the Marree Man. With its lines fading by the day, it is unlikely it will ever receive the investigation it deserves.

Crop circle enthusiasts will not be surprised at the dismissal of this huge glyph. As has been shown time and again in the croppie world, and reinforced here, just fax or e-mail a few claims and insinuations around, and many will simply accept the words before them. There is a strange willingness in some to accept the flimsiest of mundane explanations without even a whimper of further questioning if it makes the world seem cosily explicable again.

With thanks to Grace Blaker for sending Australian press cuttings (inevitably more substantial than British reports) and to David Stott of the Crossways Hotel, Wilmington, who I personally interviewed after reading local press reports.

Original article: SC, issue 83, March-April 1999

14 THE MAN FROM ATLANTIS

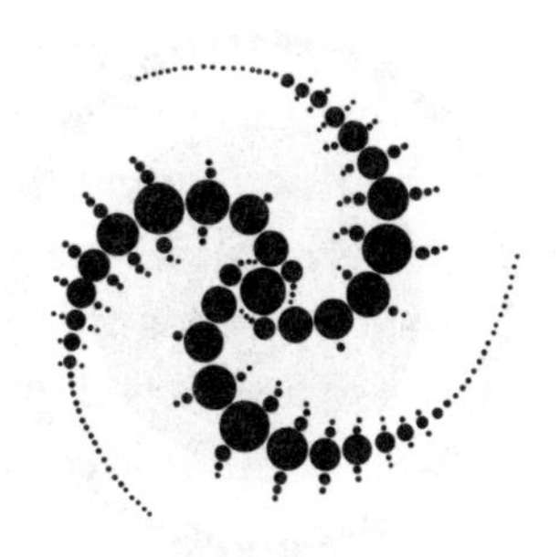

Extraordinary claims require extraordinary evidence, it is often said. Sometimes people appear on the lecture circuit bearing what seems to be such evidence. But further scrutiny must be applied when things don't add up. Here is a cautionary tale of one man who claimed he had found the lost city of Atlantis...

A few months ago, a researcher outside the croppie community, but one who has carried out scientific experiments with aspects of crop circles which have attracted burgeoning interest, gave a presentation for members of the London branch of the Centre for Crop Circle Studies. As part of his lecture, he unexpectedly announced he had been working with archaeologists investigating what have become known as the Scott Stones, off the coast of Bimini, near Miami, USA. These are underwater remains which some have stated are what is left of Atlantis, the legendary lost continent.

Our lecturer began to show actual photographs of these structures, taken by him, he claimed, whilst diving. The pictures were astonishing, provoking gasps of amazement; virtually untouched Egyptian-looking statues, sun dials, strange helmet-like devices and stone needles resting on white sands in clear blue waters, exotic fish swimming among them. He stated that these were genuine artefacts from Atlantis and that photos of them had never been shown at a presentation anywhere in the world before. He then displayed pictures of objects brought to the surface, allegedly taken at the Miami Museum of Science.

It all seemed too good to be true. Surely this was the archaeological find of the century, so why were we, a small audience of crop circle enthusiasts, being treated to such a scoop? How could the underwater pictures be so clear, the remains so untouched by time and erosion? Many times he was questioned, but he categorically claimed they were *his* photos, taken whilst diving, and that he believed this was indeed the site of Atlantis.

Discussion ran rife after the presentation, some unable to accept the reality of what had been shown. The presenter was therefore taken aback to learn that Michael Green, CCCS President and MC for the evening, was not just one of London's leading authorities on Atlantis, but also believed himself to be the reincarnation of one of the Atlantean High Priests who had presided at the time of its unfortunate demise. Indeed, the presenter seemed more than a little perturbed at this revelation. Wanting to investigate further, Michael invited the speaker to dinner the following day - where the claims were reasserted.

A few days later, several attenders of the meeting, and others who had subsequently been made aware of the Atlantis photos, were somewhat surprised by a BBC television holiday programme. The report featured a new venture for the rich - the Atlantis Paradise Island, a plush hotel on an isolated island resort shaped around the theme of Atlantis, with luxury accommodation, casinos, swimming pools - and an underwater exhibition of mock 'artefacts' viewed from a glass tunnel, known as 'The Dig'... Immediately, the resemblance to the 'Atlantis' photos seen the week before was obvious, some of the same objects clearly visible.

Confronted with this via e-mail, the presenter claimed the hotel had simply copied the real artefacts for their display. Yet no-one in the archaeological community had even heard of such a find in the first place.

Michael Green, being ex-*English Heritage*, has excellent contacts. Dissatisfied with this excuse, Michael first made enquiries at the Miami Museum of Science. It denied any knowledge of a display of Atlantean objects.

Michael then contacted the Atlantis Paradise Island for a brochure and promotional video. The brochure clearly showed what was seen in London, and the video, made before the hotel was finished, showed computer graphic versions of the glass tunnel experience, the same artefacts even present in the animations. Michael sent photocopies of photos given to him by the presenter to Franz Hepburn, Sales Manager for Sun International, the main UK contact for Atlantis Paradise Island. He responded with this statement: *"I can confirm that the photos are authentic* (sic) *and can be seen on a visit to the Atlantis Resort, Paradise Island, The Bahamas."*

When confronted with this, our presenter declined to respond further. He emigrated to Canada just months later.

It would seem that for one night a madness struck someone previously thought of as reliable and respectable. It is possible it was just a joke that got out of hand, the unexpected interest shown in London making the story hard to retract. Yet the presenter was given many opportunities to come clean, and persisted with what can only be seen as a cynical sham. Is it possible he himself had been led astray and really did think the objects at the hotel - which he must have visited or obtained photos from - actually were authentic rather than just entertainment displays? But if so, what was all this about diving amongst them? The reason for the perfection of the pictures now seems clear - they were taken through glass. And the lack of erosion in the objects is because they are only about a year old - not 12,000.

This sad episode inevitably cast doubt on the person in question's other areas of research, thus undoing the good among the bad. Certainly his crop circle findings must now be treated with caution and those who feel betrayed by what has happened have come to doubt every aspect of his alleged background and qualifications.

So, if someone at a lecture starts showing you pictures of what is claimed to be Atlantis and they look anything like that described in this piece, start heckling very loudly - or at least ask some very serious questions of your speaker...

Original article: SC, issue 85, July-August 1999

15 GALAXY LEGACY

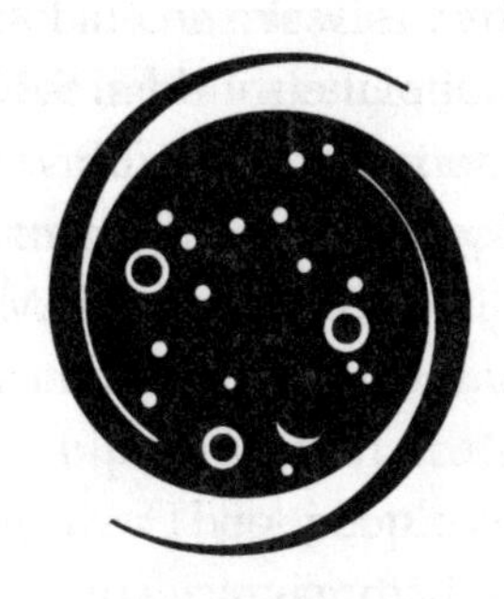

When, in 1994, three 'galaxy' crop formations, clearly meant to be read as star maps, appeared in the fields, it took several years before their meaning was realised. When it was found they were showing a planetary alignment in Cetus due to occur at midnight GMT on the 6/7th April 2000, there was a flurry of speculation as to what might occur on that date. This piece was written shortly after the date arrived, recording what transpired and providing a valuable snapshot of the feelings of expectancy at this time... (For this edit, I have resisted the temptation to change my predictions in the light of subsequent events, but have inserted updated comments where appropriate.)

So... nothing happened on the date predicted by the 1994 galaxy formations, then. Or did it? Those who think certain elements of croppiedom are desperate to find some kind of meaning to these extraordinary prescient patterns and will simply shoehorn any old thing in to fit can skip this. Those more deeply intrigued should read on...

A quick recap: in 1994, three crop formations resembling star patterns, or 'galaxies' as they were named, appeared near the Wiltshire hamlets of

West Kennett, West Stowell and Froxfield. Four years later, astronomer Jack Sullivan, in a series of articles in *SC* journal (principally *SC* 81 & 82) revealed that these patterns were in fact showing a very specific conjunction (or 'massing') of planets - Mars, Saturn, Jupiter and the Moon - which would occur in the constellation Cetus at midnight GMT on 6/7th April 2000. Other formations were also revealed as very specific planetary conjunctions (*SC* 84, 87 & 89) occurring at various dates.

But 6/7th April seemed the most urgent 'message', portrayed as it was in three separate crop patterns. What would happen? Was a supernova about to blossom in that constellation? Was the killer comet on its way that day? Was it astrologically significant? Was it only the date that mattered, not the conjunction, which might simply have been used as a date-specifier? No-one knew. Finally, a few weeks ago, the date arrived...

By chance, that night I was returning from giving a lecture in Bristol and arranged to meet Michael Glickman at his cottage in Horton, near Devizes, before returning home. On leaving the cottage at 9.15pm, in a beautifully clear deep blue sky I could see the predicted arrangement of planets superimposed above a beautiful crescent moon sinking behind trees to the west. I was distracted from getting into the car by a strange crimson red cloud which caught my eye, hanging over the northern horizon. It seemed to be an almost rectangular block of softly glowing colour, motionless, covering about an eighth of the sky. From time to time it would suddenly metamorphose into striped shafts, like beams of light, and back again.

Perturbed but curious, I drove on towards Alton Barnes. Stopping on the road overlooking the East Field - as you have to, of course - to breathe the night air of the circular heartlands, I was amazed to see the block of red had brightened considerably, still shifting periodically from sheet to shafts, this time above the darkened pinnacle of Adam's Grave. Oddly, with West Stowell just a mile away, site of the best galaxy design, I made no connection then between the crimson cloud and the date, though I had been talking with Michael about the night's significance earlier.

All along the M4, from Hungerford to Windsor, the redness was striking and must surely have distracted other drivers. Visible across such a distance, it had to be large and very high up. It occurred to me that I might be enjoying a rare sighting of the Northern Lights. It faded from vision as the M25 approached.

Ceefax news had the answer when I returned home. A large solar storm had erupted, and particles reaching the Earth's magnetosphere had indeed created the widest sighting of the aurora borealis across the UK and other parts of Europe for many years, usually being restricted to more northern regions, hence its more common name. I considered myself lucky to have witnessed it. Jack Sullivan had sat out on Ashdown Forest to view the planetary conjunction before it sank behind the horizon for its appointment with the exact time predicted by the formations, but had seen nothing in the way of auroras, though curiously others further west on the south coast *did* see it.

Perhaps unexpectedly, the planetary conjunction itself was considered remarkable enough to make it into the newspapers. One even carried a story that some believed the sudden (and, to some, suspicious) computer crash on the English stock markets on 5th April - the last day of the UK tax year - might have been caused by an unusual energy configuration generated by the astronomical alignment. Others simply ran stories about the visual beauty of the conjunction, which would *"not be repeated for 20 years"* according to the *Daily Telegraph*. In fact it's much rarer than that. In a letter written to me a few days later, Jack Sullivan wrote:

"This is a bit misleading. They mean that a conjunction of the three planets will not be repeated for 20 years. Indeed, these conjunctions happen regularly at intervals of roughly 20 years at different places on the ecliptic. The date of the next one is 27th March 2020 in Sagittarius. The Moon will then be in Eridanus, well away from the three planets. According to my computer program searches over a period of 3000 years, the recent conjunction in Cetus (or Aries) with the Moon present as we saw, will not occur again. It does indeed appear to be a unique event over a very long time."

As I began to read about the conjunction and the Northern Lights in the news from various sources over the next few days, a strange feeling began to creep up on me. The solar storm, caused by an enormous flare thrown out by the Sun as it approached its 11-year peak of sunspot activity, had been measured by some observatories as a 'G4' event on a scale of 1 to 5 - very big. Some newsgroups carried the story that it was the largest solar storm in many years, threatening satellite communications and other electronic systems.

Maybe this was what the galaxy formations were alerting us to... Was the storm important in some cryptic way? As Jack Sullivan put it: *"This very rare aurora does seem to add more significance to the conjunction event and could well have been more than just a coincidence. If so, the implications are pretty astounding."*

The Sun, or what certainly looks something like it, has featured regularly as a recurring motif in the crop circles. The 1998 'Beltane Wheel' at West Kennett, for instance, is not dissimilar to a version of the Mayan flower/sun glyph (provided by the Mayan daykeeper Hunbatz Men). The 1997 Etchilhampton 'grid' formation of 780 boxes, which some interpret as being a pointer towards the much speculated-on year 2012 (the final year portrayed in the Mayan calendar - 26 by 30 boxes could mean 26 weeks times 30, equalling 15 years. 15 years from 1997 takes you to... 2012), is accompanied by a star or sun symbol (showing the sun's six rotating magnetic fields, according to Geoff Stray - see *www.diagnosis2012.co.uk*). Numerous other crop glyphs suggest solar activity.

According to Jack Sullivan, in his article in *SC* 82, the so-called 'DNA' formation of 1996 (a double helix of circles which appeared at Alton Barnes) is closer to being a diagram of the Earth making four equinoxal processions - a four year journey - around the Sun, which, in his interpretation, makes up the central 12-circle spine of the pattern. Taking a four year period on from the date of the design's appearance (June 17th) takes us to spring/early summer this year - 2000. In 1999, a strange formation appeared at Avebury Trusloe on 23rd August, a circle with five radiating wiggly arms and a long misshapen tail. In *SC* 86 we described it as *"...looking rather like a sun giving off solar flares. Let's hope it's not a warning, as one of the arms is much longer than the other!"*

What's the big deal with the Sun though? What difference can the odd solar storm make to us? Can this really be the event the galaxy formations were signifying?

If anyone out there has a copy handy, they should check out Maurice Cotterell's book *Astrogenetics* (Western Litho, 1993). Later books by Cotterell have re-emphasised its main point in different contexts. Cotterell and others have discovered that the rising and falling of civilisations can be directly mapped against long-term cycles of sunspot activity (the short-term cycle being 11 years), which correlate precisely. The periods of *least* activity seem to produce times of cultural stagnation and low fertility, while high solar turbulence stimulates leaps in evolution due, according to Cotterell, to the action of solar radiation on human genes (this theory also neatly justifies the reality of astrological influences on character development). Cotterell writes:

"Interstellar radiation bombards the foetus at conception causing chemical reactions within the enzymes of the first living cells through the process of cellular radiobiology. Chromosomes are spliced and rearranged. The inherited genes are thus mutated... ...If excessive radiation from huge solar disturbances reached Earth, all living species would undergo a mutational leap as the Earth's geomagnetic field increased intensity. This then explains en-masse *mutational evolution."*

Is this current peak of the solar cycle (a peak in both the short-term and the long-term cycles) having a greater effect on our genes than we know? Were we, on the night predicted by the galaxy formations, flooded with something of great value to our growth as a species? Are these times, as many believe, a crucial moment in our evolution? If the solar activity of this last month was what was being signified by the galaxy crop formations, maybe it won't be a few years until we begin to see the genetic effects on the generation born at this time. It's a profound thought.

All questions, no answers. Wishy-washy speculation? Maybe, but speculation is what the crop circles have always been about and this interpretative association is about as solid as any other ever made. We risk missing potentially important realisations if we refuse to speculate. Croppies hardly have to worry about losing credibility.

If you want to stretch things really far, muse on this: the relevance of the number 11 to crop circles has been spoken of several times in recent years. It is a geometrical combination which hasn't yet been properly utilised in the mathematical construction of formations [*significantly, it finally came big-time in 2000, just weeks after this was written*]. It was hinted at last year in a couple of designs, but wasn't overt. Its full appearance would mark the first step into what Michael Glickman calls the 'Master Sequence', from 11 to 77, indicating our first foothold toward understanding and accessing 'other-dimensional realities'. If and when eleven-fold geometry does turn up in the fields, it may be no coincidence and could be a pointer. We now stand at the peak of the 11-year sunspot cycle. Its last peak was 1989, the year which seemed to close the first chapter of crop circles and made way for the extraordinary (now taken for granted) pictograms which followed in 1990. Several of those first complex patterns utilised two rows of thin rectangular boxes. These could be read as number 11s either side of a central pathway - perhaps marking the boundary of a solar cycle? The combination of 11/11 is, of course, considered very meaningful by many numerologists. The clear appearance of 11 in a crop formation at the end of this cycle (this year), or the beginning of the next (2001) might be a clue to a link between the Sun, the crop circles and our evolution [*as mentioned, eleven-fold geometry DID indeed come in 2000. Interestingly, however, the sunspot cycle was late to finish, activity usually more associated with peak-time still occurring in 2002...*]. If there is any kind of mirror to 1990's precedent as the first year after a sunspot peak, 2001 should produce a major leap forward in the development of this phenomenon... *[In fact, though there were some obvious significant developments, it was not overall the leap some expected, but as the sunspot cycle was still unexpectedly out even by 2002, maybe we still have to wait to validate this prediction.]*

We shall see. Or maybe we won't.

But if you think *that's* all baloney, the most amazing thing which happened on 6th April took place at Michael Glickman's cottage, several hours after I left that night. At about 3.00am, lights out and Glickers safely tucked up in bed, Michael's hi-fi system *turned itself on* and began blasting out John Lee Hooker at full volume... Other people we heard from after reported alarm clock radios going off around the same time.

Now *that's* weird.

Original article: SC, issue 90, May-June 1999

All will be put right on BBC Breakfast News, however. Surely? Although [illegible] the paranormal feature. It's extremely [illegible]. A few [illegible] of interviews, some crop circles. Martin gets to speak, everyone looks cheerful. [illegible] is [illegible] as the full-run is never shown in its entirety and it's only very briefly mentioned that UFO and other sightings have been made here. Still, there's Marcus, but who's that standing next to him, cape flapping in the wind? Oh God, it's the Master of Pendulums.

Marcus stands, stiffly, with his back to the Master, as if pretending not to have noticed. With trepidation, I watch as Marcus launches into his spiel about the potential of [illegible] technology, which may well constitute Japanese TV sets according to some. He [illegible] putting a fair case for ET-inspired inventions, even if Marcus is playing his usual role as Devil's advocate.

[illegible] the Master of Pendulums. Any credibility to the report dissolves instantly. The Master has a fail-safe method of communicating with ETs, he says – by playing tunes on a child's toy xylophone, duly demonstrated. My jaw drops as many fellows [illegible] sympathise with Marcus, visibly cringing next to this spectacle. It [illegible] as hell, [illegible] [illegible], but [illegible] [illegible] good television [illegible] insights [illegible]. Apparently. The [illegible] of the [illegible] [illegible] studio, the presenter [illegible] [illegible] [illegible].

We exchange [illegible] over the telephone as the morning progresses, Marcus threatening to strike off the Christmas card list anyone who ever mentions the Master of Pendulums in his presence again. According to Martin, his father-in-law, having tuned in specially, merely [illegible] to be more important than it was, didn't [illegible] [illegible] [illegible] to deflate any potential credibility to the event. [illegible]

16 DUST TO DUST

Some formations present unexpected surprises in the fine details. Who would have thought a pile of white dust found in a 2002 crop circle would create so much fuss? Though subsequent investigations into the dust threw up more questions than answers, this previously unpublished article records some of the discoveries and speculations so far...

If Alton Barnes in Wiltshire is the Mecca of the crop circle world, in terms of numbers of events and focus of interest, then Sompting near Worthing in West Sussex is the Alton Barnes of the south coast. Since 1990, so much circular activity has taken place in this square mile surrounding the ancient and unique Knights Templar church of St Mary's, that it's certainly had the lion's share of Sussex crop circles over the years. Theories vary as to why, but some dowsers of our acquaintance tell us that an important earth energy line runs down from the Iron Age hill-fort of Cissbury Ring, a few miles north-west, bangs into the church and then radiates out in smaller lines from there, feeding the neighbouring fields [*see my and Paul Bura's book* Quest For Contact *for more on this*].

So eyes are always turned towards this area when Sussex begins to come alive with its summer cerealogical offerings, and 2002 was not the first year to have Sompting deliver the first of the county batch on June 3rd. It came in the form of a marvellous ringed circle with two large but graceful curving arms, each 194 feet in length. On the night of its appearance, two children in a nearby house watched a bright light hovering over the field at about 1.00am. The field is closely surrounded by houses on three sides, with the A27 road running alongside. Though no-one else has yet recorded the light, neither has anyone reported seeing teams of people taking hours struggling to produce this masterpiece, lit up for all to see in the clear orange glow of the street lamps which illuminate the whole area.

But this formation is mentioned merely for context, and is not the focus of the piece. A while later, on June 23rd, at the northern end of the same long, long L-shaped field - almost half a mile in length - a newer sibling arrived. Taking the form of a 90 feet diameter convex triangle (ie. with curved edges) superimposed with three overlapping rings of around 82 feet diameter and other curved paths, this glyph, like its predecessor, showed a similarly fine quality to its lay in terms of intricacy, but took a different symbolic approach.

The usual investigations followed; pilots alerted for aerial surveillance, the farmer tracked down, tape measures packed into rucksacks. The whole Sompting area was well-known to us of old, of course, but this field in particular held memories. In 1993, a bizarre formation affectionately known as 'The Kebab' appeared just feet from the very same spot as this new arrival and we had conducted some experiments there. Allan Brown was the first to enter its 2002 descendent and quickly spied what looked like a splurge of white powder, or dust, in two patches a few feet across, one at the centre of the convex triangle, the other a little further to the north east. The impression was that something like a bag of flour had impacted on the crop. It lay liberally over the fallen crop, but in even thicker quantities on the soil beneath.

When I entered the formation with Allan later that same day, he called

Preparing the stage for the annual Glastonbury Symposium gathering, and the final result. *"The pictogram banners hanging from the ceiling proclaim the crop circles as its first focus and everything then moves outwards from there... ...Although crop circles are the springboard for many of the presentations, they are more often used as catalysts to open doors to much wider issues"* - from Chapter 9, *Conference Season.*
Photos: Andy Thomas

On a live BBC news report, Marcus Allen attempts to maintain composure in the face of the curse of the geriatric eccentric... *"On shuffles the Master of Pendulums. Any credibility to the report dissolves instantly. The Master has a fail-safe method of communicating with ETs, he says - by playing tunes on a child's toy xylophone, duly demonstrated..."* - from Chapter 11, *Attack of the Red Cape.* Video images courtesy of BBC Television

Croppies gather for the closing ceremony of the Wiltshire Crop Circle Celebration (images from two separate years). *"At the closing ceremony of the Alton Barnes weekend, a ring of over a hundred people stand, hands linked, watching Rod Bearcloud perform his rather beautiful ritual and haunting chant"* - from Chapter 12, *Media Scrum.*
Photos: Andy Thomas

A Japanese crew from Nippon TV maintain a watch on the fields of Alton Barnes. *"A caravanette perilously perched on the summit of wind-swept Adam's Grave... ...Sipping tea, the ad-hoc staff glance at the monitors from time to time, fed by conventional and infra-red cameras shaking outside in the permanent gale of the Pewsey Downs"* - from Chapter 12, *Media Scrum.* Photos: Andy Thomas

Steve Alexander is interviewed by the Nippon TV crew, while the BBC prowl the marquees of the Alton Barnes Crop Circle Celebration. *"Uninvited, they turn up and pin people against walls, firing questions about why they believe the circles are a genuine phenomenon and how they feel about hoaxing"* - from Chapter 12, *Media Scrum.*

Nippon photo: Karen Douglas
BBC photo: Andy Thomas

The much-maligned Millennium Dome... Its negative treatment from the press and the effect this had on public opinion has many parallels with the way the population at large has allowed its perception of crop circles to be similarly led. *"The Dome itself was a thrilling structure, more impressive in reality than in pictures, its great gantries thrusting upwards into the east London skies... ...Rainbow auras of light were splashed liberally onto the inside of the tent-like surface, creating shifting atmospheres and moods as you walked around the perimeter"* - from Chapter 18, *The Last Word.*

Photos: Andy Thomas

The discovery of a strange white dust (the author seen here inspecting it) in a crop circle at Sompting, West Sussex, 2002. The dust was found to be partially made-up of a pure form of silica. *"The impression was that something like a bag of flour had impacted on the crop. It lay liberally over the fallen crop, but in even thicker quantities on the soil beneath"* - *from* Chapter 16, *Dust to Dust.*

Aerial photo: David Russell
Internal photos: Allan Brown

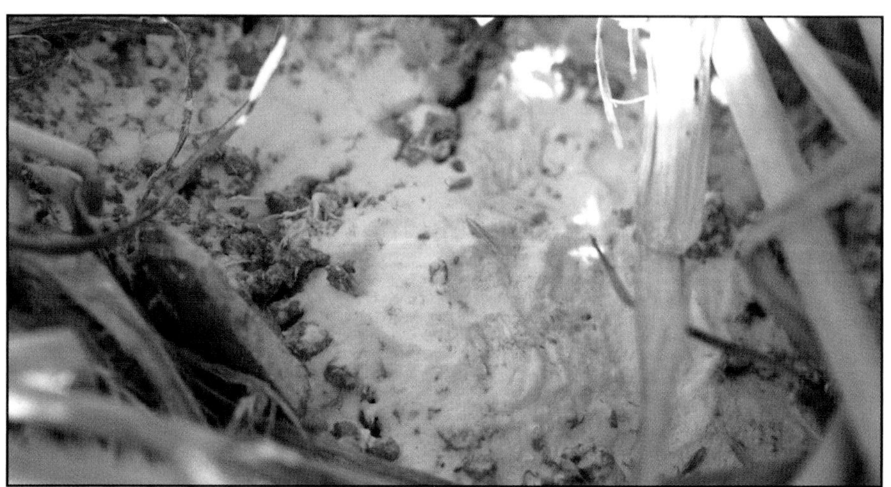

my attention to the dust. We tried to work out why someone might be throwing around white powder, and for what purpose. What was it, in any case? It was too fine and too white for flour. Talcum? But it had no scent. It seemed to just smooth itself into our fingerprints, without friction, grain or texture. I decided to take a chance and tasted a little of it. But there was no taste, giving no hint of what it might be. (Contrary to some scurrilous speculation, we did *not* attempt to sniff it through a tube of paper.)

We decided to take some samples of the dust for analysis before rain or dew washed it away, and scooped some into small sealed plastic bags.

The next question was who to send it to. The obvious answer was to approach our old friend and sometime colleague Nancy Talbott of BLT Research, the USA-based organisation sparked by the plant sample analysis of W C Levengood. The extensive work carried out by BLT has identified inexplicable biological anomalies in circle-affected crop, still unreplicated in man-made formations (see *www.bltresearch.com* for more). But in this post-September 11th world, with anthrax scares gripping the Land of the Free, and the 'War on Drugs' still running alongside the so-called 'War on Terror', was it really such a good idea to be posting white powder to the USA..? On reflection, we decided maybe not.

By telephone, Nancy recommended we contact Rodney Ashby, who had conducted UK-based analysis for her before; perhaps he could help?

Happily, Rodney, a man of scientific approach with an interest in crop circles, but not given to flights of fancy, was willing to use his professional access to something known as an EDX machine - Energy Dispersive X-ray - which could identify the elements of any given substance. We posted the samples on, and a few weeks later back came Rodney's report, edited conclusions to which follow (see footnote at the end of this article for the full text of the first paragraph):

"Elemental mapping indicated that the sample was not a mineral of complex composition, rather a mixture of three or more basic chemical compounds, the most common being the silica of the sand, then lime and slaked lime. Collectively,

these are indicative of a cementations material. This conclusion is further supported by the presence of some of the trace elements...

...Although everything pointed to a weak cement/sand mix, the problem with that conclusion was the texture of the sand, which was not a material commonly used in the building trade. Instead, it was of a finer grain size varying from 100 microns down to less than 2 microns. Also, the smaller grains were of the purest forms of silica. All the evidence suggested that the sand was from an atypical but natural source. Various ideas have been considered - sand intended for sand blasting or precision casting, even airborne Saharan sand - but none has provided a convincing match with this sample."

In other words, what we had was a mix containing a very pure form of silica, which didn't quite match with anything commonly found - something unlikely that a hoaxer would buy casually at Safeway. Despite the interesting conclusions, and his own bafflement, Rodney remained unconvinced of its importance: *"I could find no evidence to suggest that this material did not have a mundane origin."* But we had to ask ourselves; what on earth was this doing in a crop circle?

When Nancy Talbott read the full report, it was then she decided to let us in on an interesting fact - this was not the first crop circle to have produced silica deposits. She was already aware when we approached her of other reports from around the globe in past years, but didn't want to load the dice by mentioning this to either Rodney or ourselves. Now the analysis was done, it could be revealed.

So what are the silica deposits all about? Is some secret society of industrial cement aficionados at work seeking new formations and scattering substances in fields? Or could there be some atmospheric condition which lifts such silica high into the air from one location, travelling many miles before being brought down to ground level at another by the processes which might be utilised (by whatever) to create crop formations? Certainly, BLT detected deposits of meteoritic dust on some crop circles in the mid-90s, which they believed had been brought down from the ionosphere to earth by high-reaching circle-making vortices, so perhaps this idea isn't so far-fetched. But it seems hard to know for sure.

During the circle conference season of 2002, I selectively presented the white dust findings to a number of croppie gatherings, to mounting interest. Allan and I deliberately withheld from saying too much about the subject on the Internet, lest it put mischievous ideas into already mischievous heads (it probably will now).

As a result of the presentations, I began to receive suggestions from people as to what the silica might be. One woman said it was not unlike a type of borax she used in jewellery making, for instance, giving me a sample for comparison; though similar, it was not quite the same as our dust.

Marcus Allen of *Nexus Magazine* made an interesting observation that our finding recalled the 'white powder gold' written about recently in Sir Laurence Gardner's books. This was a mysterious substance known to the ancients, which was believed to have astonishing life-enhancing properties, and which was known to have contained silica as one of its constituents. When Marcus approached Sir Laurence about this possible connection, he was far from dismissive. Though Rodney Ashby's analysis showed some differences to white powder gold, Sir Laurence pointed out that what he describes as the 'Monatomic-state elements' present in white powder gold would not necessarily be revealed in the type of typical EDX test carried out on our crop circle dust, if only operated at its most basic level. In an e-mail, he wrote:

"Monatomic-state elements have boiling points way above those of the individual metals from which they derive, and they will not dissolve under any circumstances in any known acid. So if gold (with, say, a 1% aluminium impurity) is transposed into a monatomic state, initial tests will reveal only that the resultant white powder sample is aluminium. Eventually, if the tests are progressed beyond that they will reveal absolutely nothing else in the sample for a very long time...

...If Andy's material (an equivalently impalpable white powder to M-state

elements) is registering silica and aluminium qualities, but actually resembles neither to the vision or the touch, then there's a very good chance that his powder is an M-state element - most probably one of the platinum group metals: platinum, palladium, iridium, rhodium, ruthenium or osmium."

These thoughts led Sir Laurence to put forward a crop circle hypothesis of his own, which might explain the dust found in some crop formations:

"Superconductive flux tubes between anywhere in space and the earth's atmosphere will theoretically remain in a fairly constant position, but small variations in the earth's own movement could cause them to hit the ground (when activated) at variable spots within generally predictable regions (where there is high energy superconductivity of some sort below ground) at certain times of the solar year.

*Flux tube frequencies (just like DNA or computer graphics) can be expressed mathematically, and in visual terms those mathematics can convert to pure geometry. Flux tube frequencies [*as explained in Sir Laurence's book *Lost Secrets of the Sacred Ark] can and will superconduct extraterrestrial M-State elements, depositing them either in our own familiar space-time dimension or some other.*

...Maybe what we have are naturally occurring flux tubes activated by whatever means at certain times of year to ground themselves in specific places. Their mathematics might then be expressed as a pure geometry that would vary every time in accordance with the superconductive frequency waves of the instant."

Aside from Sir Laurence's fascinating theories, a number of others pointed out a possible link to the rectangular crop formation which had appeared alongside a pixellated humanoid face near the Chilbolton (Hampshire) radio telescope in 2001. This glyph was a mutated version of a binary message Mankind had beamed out into space as an experimental transmission in 1974, giving details to hypothetical extra-terrestrials of such things as our DNA structure, chemical elements, planetary position and global population. The Chilbolton 'reply' formation presented details of a different lifeform from humanity... Curiously, it also added in sili*con* as an extra element in the relevant part of the chart - could this also have meaning?

All these possible connections and suggestions were truly compelling, but, as ever, provided only tantalising titbits, difficult to prove.

Eventually, one other attractive idea came in an e-mail I received from Jim Lyons, a remarkable and open-minded physicist and one time scientific officer for the Centre for Crop Circle Studies. He attached an interesting study of ball lightning by John Abrahamson of the University of Canterbury in Christchurch, New Zealand, which Jim felt might have relevance. Essentially, the report was recording similar silica deposits being left in association with the appearance of ball lightning - weather-related globes of plasma which bear a striking resemblance to some of the balls of light witnessed many times in and around crop formations. Jim wrote:

"I have had a look at Rodney's charts. The bulk spectral curve is very interesting - exactly what I would expect. The two key elements are silicon & oxygen; these would be anticipated if a rising plasma source had broken down quartz (silica). The high level of calcium is also consistent with the underground chalk. This would be present if energy had come up through the ground. My gut feeling is that you have something significant here which could help verify Abrahamson's hypothesised model... ...This is the first indication I have seen which could possibly support Abrahamson`s model of a rising plasma energy source involving observed lights. It is by no means proof as it stands, but does point us in the right direction.

The oxide extracted from the soil on Abrahamson's model is silicon dioxide - quartz in other words, commonly found under crop formations. Oxidation of the quartz due to the plasma ball would leave silicon - I guess in powdered form."

So we had another interesting lead - could the silica deposits be due to the impacting of the balls of light some believe play a major role in the creation of crop circles? Rodney Ashby was less sure, however, writing:

"Well... I agree with the second sentence; the composition is 'exactly what I would expect'. Oxygen, calcium and silicon are the most common elements at the surface of the earth's crust. They are ubiquitous, so it is not surprising that they should be commonly found under crop formations...

...This sort of talk about rising plasma energy is not science as I recognise it. Actually, if you stop to think about it, the earth is a fairly good conductor and would short out any sort of plasma which is, after all, just circulating current.

Finally, he [Jim] *says: Oxidation of the quartz due to the plasma ball would leave silicon. Actually, quartz is an oxide. It's just one of several forms of the dioxide, others being tridymite and cristobalite. Silicon is the element and it cannot be produced by heating quartz in air - even by plasma.*

So this seemed to squash a promising idea - but who was right? By now we were out of our depth. It was time to leave the scientists to argue among themselves. More, much more, work needs to be done in this area. We hope someday that the mystery of the white dust will be investigated further. Indeed, it is hoped that the publication of this article will encourage further delving by other interested parties.

As a little coda, it's worth relating that one or two other people also took samples of the silica. 2012 expert and SCR colleague Geoff Stray had scraped up some examples for himself and carried a little paper sachet around in his wallet for the summer. At the *Galatea* cafe one night of the Glastonbury Symposium, conversation turned to our white dust, following a presentation by Allan Brown and myself. When Geoff declared his sachet for inspection, there was great excitement as it was passed around the table. In a moment recalling the famous coke-sneezing scene in Woody Allen's *Annie Hall*, one casual cough and a flick from an interested party quickly saw the entire contents scattered across the table and floor... It's nice to know that somewhere in microscopic recesses of the wooden tables and floorboards of a cafe in Glastonbury lie the remnants of a curious substance which once appeared in a mystery glyph from a field 200 miles away... wherever that substance came from.

FOOTNOTES:

The full text of the first paragraph to Rodney Ashby's main conclusions to his analysis reads:

"The elemental composition suggested that only oxides or hydroxides (note that no hydrogen peak appears in an EDX trace. Boron is the lightest element normally detectable) were present. Elemental mapping indicated that the sample was not a mineral of complex composition, rather a mixture of three or more basic chemical compounds, the most common being the silica SiO2 of the sand, then lime CaO and slaked lime Ca(OH)2. Collectively, these are indicative of a cementations material. This conclusion is further supported by the presence of some of the trace elements. For example, calcium aluminate Ca2Al2O5 and trace compounds of alumina and iron are constituents of Portland cement."

In a later communication, Rodney goes on to say:

"There was considerable variation in the purity and texture of the grains... ...It's this variation that makes it difficult to identify a single source. It's a bit like sand that has accumulated in the bed of a river having come from various upstream rock-strata. As a matter of fact, a very high proportion of the grains had rounded contours, suggesting that they had been smoothed by the action of water and this rounding could even help to account for the smooth feel of the material."

Referring to the John Abrahamson ball lightning report, Jim Lyons adds:

*"There has been a dramatic change in attitude from Science towards the concept of ball lightning. The January 2002 issue of the Proceedings of the Royal Society was entirely devoted to ball lightning and related effects. Included in the issue were anecdotal quotes from several people around the world. This is an enormous breakthrough in terms of scientific reporting! The outcome of all this latest modelling is that there appear to be techniques whereby balls of light can sustain their appearance for longer than just a few seconds. Previous to this, one dare not mention BOLs [*Balls of Light*] in mainstream scenarios."*

Previously unpublished.

17 CRIMES OF THE SIGNS

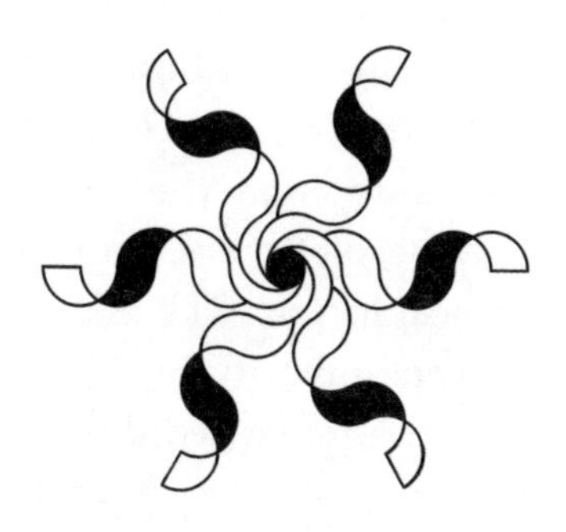

In 2002, Hollywood finally caught up with the fictional potential of crop circles with the arrival of the movie Signs, *starring Mel Gibson battling crop-vandalising, water-fearing aliens. Despite its simplistic and, for some, crass portrayal of the circle phenomenon, the film hugely raised its public profile after several fallow years...*

A bus has just gone by. On the surface, not much of a moment to report, but this bus is different. As I sit with Allan Brown and Martin Noakes in a Brighton pizza cafe, animatedly discussing the pluses and minuses of *Signs,* which we have just viewed at a press preview screening with a handful of local journalists and other interested parties, it drives by, with a golden pictogram adorning its side. Crop circles. On a bus. Think about it.

This is one of the effects of *Signs*. The circles may simply be advertising the film, but this is vastly symbolic of what Hollywood's rather Johnny-come-lately interest in the phenomenon is doing - spreading the word that there is something strange out there in the fields, on a scale that no enthusiast website, book or conference could ever attain in these cynical times. It's a fictional pictogram on the bus, for sure, and Hollywood cares not one jot about promoting the real thing, but from the newly raised awareness, particularly in America, that such things really ARE occurring, there has been a significant leap of interest that is not to be sniffed at, whatever the merits or otherwise of the film itself and despite the rather unfortunate connection with the concept of evil aliens.

Many croppies have made clear their feelings about *Signs*, its misrepresentations and gaping plot holes, through numerous comments and articles in the cerealogical forum. The majority vote appears to be a thumbs down, but a significant minority have leapt to its defence.

Essentially, the plot can be summarised thus: clergyman (Mel Gibson) loses faith after wife is rather gruesomely squashed by car - crop circles appear in nearby field and across world - UFOs appear over cities - tall green aliens appear and try to "harvest" people - ex-clergyman's family are trapped in house, pursued by alien - clergyman's boy has near-fatal asthma attack - alien is clubbed to death by baseball bat - boy recovers - clergyman recovers faith.

I tried, as much as possible, to wipe my mind of preconceptions when I entered the cinema. I already knew the story (such as it is), the set-up and the outcome from at least two dozen cerealogical commentators, and had to shake off the weight of this, yet oddly, it was easy when it came to it. I took it as it came and largely forgot I had ever heard anything about it. Others had done the grinding of teeth for me over the distortions of the true phenomenon, and I was able to get on with seeing what was there.

In truth, there are many different ways this movie could have been worse for the circle-minded. In conversation afterwards, the manager of the cinema expressed surprise to me that the movie confirms the phenomenon as a non-human enigma. It was his full expectation that the whole thing would turn out to be some kind of human twist, in a kind of *Scooby-Doo* "you-meddling-kids" revelation. He seemed shocked that the movie allowed the circles to be firmly placed in the pantheon of the paranormal. This must be a major surprise to many other viewers. It is also, for the croppie, the big mitigating factor that really ought to muffle some of the knee-jerk condemnation. The association with a nasty threat from outer space is a problem, but at least the circle phenomenon is portrayed as being REAL, and the doubters, given a little space early on, are seen to be wrong. This is a big step when looked at in context with the mass-media's usual sceptical dismissal.

Of the doubter's comments, however, there is one classic statement that surely all circle enthusiasts must learn by heart from now on, to cheer them up during the next inevitable media debunk. It comes when Joaquin Phoenix remarks of the human circlemakers that they are simply "Nerds who can't get girlfriends". Remember that one.

Some of the notions about the circles are quaintly warped from the reality, of course. We learn, for instance, from TV broadcasts, of the flurry of formations which appear across the world all in one night (an occurrence genuinely hoped for by many cerealogists, eager to silence doubters, alas, as yet unfulfilled), and that the phenomenon was thought to have died out in the early 80s, when, of course, in truth it first came to big attention then and built up to a huge explosion of formations in England throughout the 1990s. No reference is made to this, as if the movie hopes to gain, drama-wise, by pretending nothing in the real history of crop circles has ever occurred. Indeed, England, the very heart of the real phenomenon, is only acknowledged onscreen as having just ONE formation (curiously listed as being at 'Wakefield' - an insider joke about one-time croppie videomaker Grant Wakefield, perhaps, who has movie industry contacts?).

The crop formations shown on the TV bulletins (which, rather cheaply, are our only window onto the rest of the world's peril throughout the whole movie) are all genuinely recorded patterns, but re-labelled as if they had appeared around the world. Curiously, nearly ALL the formations shown are from 1990, including amongst them the first Alton Barnes pictogram. None of the later mandalas or geometric forms are shown, as if the filmmakers fear this might confuse viewers, for whom the early 90s forms, strung out length-wise with their 'claws' and rectangular boxes, still make up the archetypal perception of a crop formation.

The pictogram which troubles Mel Gibson's family is, in fact, little to write home about, and, apart from the fact that it's laid in the unusual choice of maize, would probably rate as one of the lesser-formations of any season these days were it to appear outside of celluloid. It's not even particularly well-filmed, the one aerial zoom-out shot of it looking dark and dowdy (as does much of the rest of the film, which revels in its visual and contextual gloom). The new UK movie poster makes much more of the formation than the film does, lit in mysterious golden sunlight and long shadows, which one might have thought a more appropriate treatment onscreen, but it is not to be. As for the lay, I found myself getting worryingly into anorak mode when I heard the characters saying, awestruck, "it's bent, not broken...", and found myself looking closely and thinking, well that stalk looks broken to me, and that one looks a bit scuffed... etc. But that's what eleven years of field work does for you, I'm afraid. I'm taking tablets for it.

However, the most important thing here is the word "awestruck", and that's why I find myself forgiving the movie many sins that might otherwise cause serious niggles. The crop formations are shown to be things treated not with ridicule, but with AWE, which is the correct treatment for these astonishing patterns which have transfixed us for so long. The regrettable taint of fear which comes with this - the formations are essentially, if somewhat mundanely, landing beacons for evil alien craft - is the big disappointment. But the awe demonstrated gains back some points.

What has inevitably most alarmed croppies so far is that FEAR is the big factor in the movie. If someone wanted to engender fear of extra-terrestrial presences into the population, they couldn't have pushed many more buttons than are pressed in *Signs*. The overall tone is one of misery, as signified by the greys and browns which permeate the movie and make the downbeat beiges of Woody Allen pictures look radiant in comparison. Any opportunity for jokes here about 'greys' are quashed by the fact that the aliens are, in fact, somewhat unimaginatively, green and tall, recalling 50's movies like *Invaders from Mars*. Indeed, the first sight we get of one of the alien 'raiders' (rather than invaders - it is postulated at the end that the attack on earth is simply some sort of quickie human larder raid), is actually laughable (a kid's party is interrupted by its arrival), which is unfortunate as laughter is clearly NOT the intention of the director M Night Shyamalan for the most part. Fear and suspense pervades, despite the odd flash of intentional humour. I'll leave it to the professional conspiracy theorists to draw their own conclusions here as to the film's message for humanity and what we should do if aliens really do arrive (clue: have a baseball bat at hand). Allan Brown has also pointed out an interesting analogy of America's current foreign policy and its 'War on Terrorism' to the behaviour shown here - the siege mentality of boarding up the windows against a perceived big outside threat, repelling external influences, but striking out decisively when required.

Quite what the aliens are 'harvesting' from humanity - it is suggested they want us for food - isn't really clear, but if, as shown in *Signs*, the aliens descend only where they've put a crop circle down first, then it's probably safe to say that the villagers of Alton Barnes and Avebury probably would have provided the heftiest lunch of all (were it not for the fact that England has largely been disinherited in the film - another interesting analogy).

The story seems primarily concerned with being a parable about personal faith. The foibles, holes and inconsistencies of the movie's actual plot have already been mightily investigated and roundly savaged by croppies (aliens which can be destroyed easily by a few water drops choose to attack a planet *covered* in water?), and there seems little need to go over them here, suffice to say that thinking too deeply about the whole scenario of the aliens' motives and seemingly bizarre way of implementing them is inadvisable. It's the movies.

It has already been suggested by more than one observer that this movie is really the flip side of *Close Encounters of the Third Kind*. Indeed, the vast majority of *Signs* is essentially a vast-elongation of the first half of the Spielberg epic, but with light replaced by dark and without that story's transfiguring resolution. There's even a scene where Gibson begins to get weird with food, *a la* Richard Dreyfuss. Indeed, *Signs* seems to lack resolution all round. The movie progresses to nothing more than the economical people-trapped-in-an-elevator syndrome, stuck firmly within the confines of one house for almost half its length. There's barely a mention - and certainly not a proper portrayal - of the effects of the alien raid on the rest of humanity, short of snippets snatched on TV and radio. Agreed, the intention seems partly to look at the very personal effect such an alien visitation might have on one family, and suspense is accordingly cranked up, fairly successfully, but after a while the claustrophobia becomes stifling rather than exciting, and in the end the climax results in nothing more spectacular than a *Goodfellas*-style baseball bat attack and some glasses of water being thrown around.

For all this, *Signs* works on some levels. It would take a brick not to feel some twinge of emotion when we witness, in flashback, Gibson's screen wife giving her last words whilst sandwiched between a truck and a tree, and it must be said that Gibson does a pretty good job with his moody hang-dog expressions and father-in-distress wranglings. Even the kids manage to engage rather than irritate, most of the time anyway, and Joaquin Phoenix provides younger hunk value. Unusually, the temptation to add in a busty damsel in distress is avoided completely here. Indeed, apart from a fairly minor friendly-neighbourhood-policewoman and the little girl, it's a very male film all round. Schmaltz does threaten once or twice, but is soon put aside once dealt with, even if fear is its replacement. There is some genuine excitement too, even if, ultimately, little develops from it.

Once the disappointment subsides that the joy and radiance inspired by the real phenomenon is not remotely touched on here, what *Signs* will be remembered for by circle enthusiasts in years to come will be its clarion call to vast sections of western society hitherto unexposed to the crop circles. It will launch - has launched - many into the knowledge that they really *are* out there, albeit in a different guise and with a seemingly benevolent quality besmirched by this Hollywood take on it. The fear-factor may repel some from wanting to know more, but there can be little doubt that with the US having made *Signs* one of its big box office hits of the year, the amount of people turned onto awareness of the crop circle phenomenon has quadrupled in the States, as website hit-rates strongly indicate. The UK effect will be much less, because the circles are already taken for granted as a seasonal happening and the British have an innate cynicism and the likes of Doug Bower still on their shores, but even here there will be new converts to interest, if the debunkers don't get to them first.

Indeed, the debunkers have much to fear from this film, which may have set their cause back for a little while, hence their current media fightback. Fears for the trivialisation of the phenomenon because of *Signs* are certainly not unfounded, and may yet come horribly true, but for a short time, at least, there is new attention and that's something to be celebrated, despite the regrettable negative associations.

The acid test for croppies has to be what people pouring out of the multiplexes will think about crop circles after this. Could it be that next time one or two hear about the phenomenon genuinely appearing in fields around them, they might give it a second thought they perhaps would not have done without the little spark of memory of a film in which the circles heralded big things? *Signs* has put crop circles on buses. Even the fear engendered in the film has one tiny redemptive feature - it at least means the formations are shown some awe and respect in the fictional world, a respect they are largely denied by most in our own reality.

For this, whatever its many flaws, *Signs* deserves a little forgiveness.

Original article: www.swirlednews.com, September 2002

18 THE LAST WORD

How will the crop circles be looked back on by history? Why have they been so savagely criticised with such a disproportionate intensity? How can those branded as 'believers' ensure the legacy of this remarkable phenomenon goes on, and stand up to the never-ending sceptical attacks? Here, then, is a last will and testament, originally written as the final piece of the final SC *journal...*

A phenomenon of beauty to a few, a pointless blot on the landscape to most others. An enclosure of sacred space or a human folly. A symbol of hope? A meaningless joke?

Yes, the Millennium Dome, Tony Blair's bequeathed gift to the British nation, generated critical dismissal like no other public happening in living memory. Except perhaps crop circles.

There are certainly many cerealogical lessons to be learned from looking at the treatment metered out to the Dome from the ever-negative British public. It was intended as a symbol of humankind's achievements, the apogee of exhibition halls and modern architecture, a place of celebration to unite technology and the soul - and, of course, prove Britain was still 'Great', by the demonstrative ability to build such a monumental edifice. How proud we would all be!

Anyone on the UK side of the Atlantic knows the overwhelming reception the Dome actually had - scepticism, cynicism, dark critical reviews bordering on hatred, and consequently public indifference (and this despite the fact it was, in terms of visitor numbers, the country's most successful attraction of the year). For one long year, the Dome was the ultimate media cannon fodder, portrayed as an unhideable empty symbol to the squandered resources of a government the press had been just waiting to pounce on after the initial euphoria of New Labour's landslide election in 1997. The Dome was the perfect chink in the armour.

The Dome, as an attraction at least, was to be open for just a single year. As autumn 2000 came and the much-desired demise of 'Blair's folly' drew ever closer, I found myself wondering whether I had been told the truth about it. Should I check it out myself, just to formulate my own opinion? Everyone seemed to *have* an opinion on the Dome, after all - despite the fact that only a handful of those mouthing them had actually been there. My cue to go came when attending a live audience debate with Michael Grade, one-time controller of the Channel 4 TV station, and well-known media mogul. As a director of the Dome, he was grilled as to his real feelings about it - but his support remained firm. I sensed a light behind his eyes when he spoke of his charge - it was clear he genuinely *believed* in it.

So, with just weeks to closure, my family and I set off one early December weekday to explore the Dome for ourselves and make up our own minds.

And it was, of course, wonderful.

Flawed? In places, yes, and clearly financially mismanaged, but a towering achievement all the same, in more ways than one. The Dome itself was a thrilling structure, more impressive in reality than in pictures, its great gantries thrusting upwards into the east London skies. But only inside did the scale of the place hit - a massive enclosure, filled with a fantastic assortment of colourful architecture which dazzled and dizzied, inducing a euphoric vertigo as one gazed up at it. Rainbow auras of light were splashed liberally onto the inside of the tent-like surface, creating shifting atmospheres and moods as you walked around the perimeter. The central auditorium itself was perhaps the most breathtaking aspect, a vast spacious womb, enclosed by draped blue curtains which soared upwards to radiating petals of steel. Some indoor structures entomb and deaden, but not the Dome - this truly felt like a sacred space had been created, a vibrant, tingly interior, where magic could happen.

Some who could agree with this might feel the educational exhibits, running the gamut of human experience, didn't live up to the magical space created for them, and there is some truth here. Too much of it had a whiff of corporate exhibition, a sense that something profound was being reached for by some of the 'zones', but compromised by (well-publicised) bad management, lack of time (the Dome was rushed into existence) or true commitment - though given its press even before it opened, the collective mind hardly aided this.

But the Dome had *heart*. Its flaws were more than made up for by the structure itself - and the Millennium Show, which took place three times a day, every day. A vast auditorium demands a big show to fill it, and the temptation to mount a crowd-pleasing empty spectacle to keep the kiddies happy must have been great. Instead, something far deeper was presented, a beautiful, stunning ballet of aerial high-wire dance and acrobatic mime, with sound and light, telling a story of the struggle between nature, technology and the spirit, as the sky people meet the earth people and attempt to meld their cultures and skills. Backed by Peter Gabriel's moving and totally appropriate music, the show brought genuine tears to the eyes and I can still feel a lump in my throat when I recall it now.

But in the weeks after my visit, I was troubled. Was I being delusional? Had I kidded myself? Was I just playing Devil's Advocate, sympathetically backing the poor loser by voicing support in the face of abusive cynicism? I had to find out, and that meant going back. With just three days left before its doom, I returned to the Dome with my family the morning after Boxing Day. I was reassured - my memory hadn't lied. For all its faults, I was in love with the Dome. I watched the show twice more, each time equally enrapt, and walked around the edifice with the same sense of awe. My task there was now complete and I returned home content, even as the bidding vultures began to move in to downgrade the Dome into mundanity [*though tragically, by 2003, the Dome was still sitting empty, rotting, after appallingly mismanaged government attempts at selling it*].

Now, you may think all this over the top. You may even have visited the Dome yourselves and disagree with me. You may think I am a sad sycophant playing with flowery language. *But are you going to deny the reality, for me, of what I experienced?*

Seeing the crop circle metaphor yet? Of course.

I was not alone in my support for the Dome. My sometime colleague Barry Reynolds had also been impressed, and after my first visit we urged attenders at the December 2000 Southern Circular Research meeting to get down to Greenwich while the chance was still there. Rolling eyes and amused tuts came from some. We asked if they had been - sheepishly, they admitted they had not. Shame on you if you ever found yourself doing the same, because by this you committed the very crime which has condemned and stigmatised the crop circle phenomenon to the outer fringes of ridicule.

The negative attitudes projected from positions of total ignorance, which condemned the Dome's reputation to a slow, agonising death, are exactly the same as those which have dogged the crop circle phenomenon since the days of Doug and Dave. The public forever give their powers of discernment and observation away to others. Many croppies do, too.

You are reading this piece and presumably don't now stand fully on the ignorant side of the fence when it comes to the circles, whatever your opinions of them, so why do you need to know this?

I have often mused over what final thought I should want to leave, if I ever had to impart one on the crop circles before some imminent demise. My work with Southern Circular Research and our journal *SC* was a prop for many over the years, helping them through times of the most hideous lies and misperceptions about the circle phenomenon from the media and public opinion. Always we have sought to counter this by actually *informing* and daring to speak out against sometimes mischievous, sometimes simply misplaced pronouncements and assertions, often from within our own cerealogical community. We know from the numerous letters and comments we have received over the last decade that we have been a great encouragement, particularly in those darker moments of doubt which some can't help themselves almost succumbing to in the face of huge media scams. But individuals need to learn to stand on their own feet. Everyone who feels drawn to this mystery owes it to themselves to stay informed and remain steady in their chosen positions against all the flak which will surely come. The strength will be there, if you really believe something of importance is happening out in the fields.

Note "something of importance". Croppies have often been portrayed and dismissed by outside foes as delusional 'believers' - that word! We have been accused of trying to set up a "pseudo-religious" cult from which no fall from blind faith into hoax heresy can be countenanced, promoting celestial circlemakers as spiritual saviours and waiting for the little green men to come down and save us all. But this is a hideous and inaccurate generalisation - the fact is, nobody knows what makes the crop circles, nor why, if there even is a why. That is the honest truth. Most croppies accept that there are some man-made formations, as they always have done. But we do NOT accept that explains the whole phenomenon. We simply believe *something of importance* is occurring, wherever it comes from. We don't need to go over the theories and their pros and cons here. There are myriads of journals, websites, books and videos which neatly take care of that.

So why the continued acid against hoax theorists? The big problem many croppies *do* have with the continual promotion of hoaxing as being the answer to the mystery from the media and some alienated sections of the crop circle community itself, is that, even apart from displaying often massive ignorance, sheer stupidity and another kind of self-delusion, it trivialises *the reality of people's personal experiences.*

There are many, many folk out there who have had their lives transformed by the presence of these strange glyphs, had epiphanies that might forever have eluded them without the catalyst of the circles, and experienced weird and wonderful phenomena. Each time the media, the sceptics or hoax claimants carp, criticise and attack with the usual sneer of self-satisfaction, they are spitting in the faces of those who have seen the doors to some kind of heaven. Why should these people's experiences be denied or ridiculed?

Increasingly aware, perhaps, of this jarring point, there have been feeble attempts by the hoax claimants and the more numerous hoax apologists, particularly of late, to change their claimed rationale, stating that the crop circles are made as 'spiritual machines' to stimulate the soul, or 'phenomena attractors' to generate strange effects by the power of shape alone, intended to harm or fool no-one. This attempt at saintly self-presentation might wash if this attitude were borne out by their behaviour, but in most cases it so obviously isn't. Too often, if commercial money-making isn't the object, we see instead clear attempts at mischief, dark deception and lies, and the betrayal of friends. The sheer relish at the fun of robbing the faithful of their vision of a mysterious and wonderful Universe is all too obvious, as claimants unveil their few openly 'human-facilitated' efforts and imply authorship of the rest thereby. The recent antics of one planker is a fine example - his unexpected criminal conviction for making just one fairly unimpressive formation has seen him produce endless e-mails of self-justification and martyred bleeding heart testimonies to media and researchers, stating how he only wanted to show that man himself could create phenomena-attracting beauty in the fields. But this cannot offset all the deception, aggressive e-mails, written threats to "destroy" the credibility of the circles, and fractious behaviour which so obviously rob his statements of any sincerity. Most 'human facilitators' simply do not generate the light around them that one would expect if their intentions were spotless, nor do they treat the phenomenon with the sense of the sacred you would feel their position would demand if claimed motivations were true.

In my book *Vital Signs*, I wrote of hoaxers:

"For a few, perhaps art and the need to create really does play a role in their motivation - but the messages they give out in their behaviour suggests less integrity. Too many opportunities have been missed to demonstrate either their commitment to inspiring beauty or the exact abilities with which to pursue it".

I accept that a good man-made formation could possibly affect someone as much as one of another origin if the undiscerning visitor didn't know which was which - but to the discerning eye, man-made demonstrations continue to fall far short of what these people should be capable of if their claims are true, and I still stand by that paragraph.

The sadness is the amount of people who fall for the apparent charisma of these ego-fired claimants, and the catchment of researchers who have allowed their initially genuine work to be diverted and mutated, from a fear of being 'caught out' in public. Better to be seen to accommodate the hoax community in the name of balance, they protest - but, of course, there is no balance; the habit of accommodating becomes an obsession, over-exposure to weasel words eat into their brains and they nearly always fall permanently into the sceptic camp in the end.

The debunk scams of Doug and Dave and those who followed in the early 90s began the rot, as the big researchers of the day suddenly became reluctant to show their true opinions for fear of being humiliated by the media. We at Southern Circular Research (beginning as a CCCS branch) had a baptism of fire and came in just as the Doug and Dave furore was at its height. Thus we actually *started* from a position of being under attack, never knowing any (largely mythical) 'golden age' of harmony and balance. Consequently we had nothing to lose and were not embarrassed to declare our belief in a real phenomenon - there were no pedestals to be toppled from.

It's easy now to underestimate the impact that new post-Doug and Dave influx of young researchers had on the old ways of cerealogy. We rattled the old established 'names' and actively campaigned against some of them as was necessary, as their failure to 'solve' the mystery (as some of them had clearly expected to) turned to rampant scepticism and bitter resentment of the optimistic new croppies. *SC* and its creators were denounced several times from live platforms, for instance, but each time it just reinforced the growing significance of the new movement. And where are the denouncers today? Largely gone or rendered impotent by their own devices. The longevity of the second generation of researchers who remain unjaded, campaigning still, now far exceeds the active interest periods of the 'golden age' predecessors.

There comes a time when ancestors have to be consigned to history and things must move on. And, inevitably, this is now happening with some of the second generation of croppies, too, and that is *alright*. It's progress of thought, development. Stand back, then, and assess with your own clear heads - those who have gone before may not hold all the answers. The mystery remains unsolved, does it not? Listen carefully to all that is said and done in the name of crop circle research and see how it feels to you. Above all, *do not give your powers of evaluation away to those who may simply* APPEAR *to be in the know*. Remember the Millennium Dome. But, then again, don't listen to me.

The world of cerealogy has been filled with very BIG pronouncements and claims from charismatic figures over the years, both non-sceptical and sceptical. Of those pronouncements, only a few have ever turned out to have any substance. Beware those who use phrases like "*I do assure you...*", but won't then give you the evidence. Claims made without evidence are as a riverbed without water; dry, arid and useless.

Use your brains! What do *YOU* think of a formation? Does its beauty or structure speak to you? What do *YOU* think of a cerealogical assertion or theory? Does it seem to have validity or substance? If you have a viewpoint, then congratulations, you are as informed on crop circle origins as any other person on the planet. Other researchers may have more facts and figures than you, but the truth is everyone is in the dark when it comes to explaining this phenomenon; it's all speculation. So when you hear someone state that 95% of formations are man-made, ask how they *KNOW*. When you hear that 35% of formations are made by kinetic mass-energy vectorisers or whatever, ask for evidence. If Joe Bloggs tells you he knows that this formation is man-made but that one isn't, ask him why he's so sure. You'll never get a straight answer, because rumours in the crop circle world are hardly ever verified and 'litmus tests' will forever be argued over. So walk away from all these people, go to the pub, have a chat with your friends and invent your own ideas. They'll be of equal worth. But don't then impose them on others. Offer them, perhaps, but don't pronounce. Similarly, listen to what other researchers have to say, read their books, enjoy their lectures, whatever, but keep your own counsel and powers of judgement.

The best and purest thing we can do is simply *inform* those who will listen of what is going on in the fields. Show them the photos and watch them gasp. Take them to the fields and see the jaws drop. And then leave them to it. It's the only responsible thing to do.

The mission to inform is not always a smooth path, of course - sometimes you have to fight for your beliefs when foes threaten. As Ian Macdonald writes in his *Beatles* book *Revolution in the Head*:

"For better or worse, it is impossible to conduct a revolution without picking a side and pointing out the drawbacks of its rivals."

Or as the poet John Milton expressed it:

"Where there is much desire to learn, there, of necessity, will be much arguing, much writing, many opinions. For opinion is but knowledge in the making."

So, fights over truth aside, even the power and ego struggles which have afflicted the cerealogical community since the earliest days, or the eternal conflict between sceptics and believers (let's call them 'positivists' - there's a new term for you) have not been wasted. I don't see these cerealogical tussles, as some do, as being an aberration in what was 'meant' to be a perfect and pure phenomenon. If anything deliberately *planned* the crop circles, and the 'sky people' are attempting to meet the 'earth people', they must have known what would result and how human nature would react.

I used to be chairman of a Brighton opera company and the in-fighting and back-stabbing there was equally bad, I can tell you. No, the slagging and slating of views and characters must always have been anticipated to be part of the scheme from any intelligent mind.

The epic sci-fi TV series *Babylon 5* had an interesting slant on this idea; the galaxy is being torn apart by a vast struggle between the Vorlons (apparently angelic beings) and the Shadows (apparently evil, insect-like demons), each sponsoring different races to support them in their eternal strife. After endless battles and disasters on an inter-planetary scale, a representative of the Shadows finally sits down and explains the reason why all this is kept going. It turns out that the Shadows and Vorlons have a joint agenda - to stimulate the evolution of galactic life through the innovation and needs created by conflict.

This is not to justify the continuing need for such conflict in our real world, but it at least gives some sense of reason as to what these comparatively mild cerealogical wranglings might have been about. In the croppie arena, we choose our sides and fight our battles according to what feels best, and the ultimate realities, which no-one can seem to pin down on either side, neither sceptics, positivists, scientists or New-Agers, are almost irrelevant. And maybe that's okay. If it feels good to believe something, then believe it. Author Richard Bach uses the phrase *"believing in things because they're fun to believe in"*. It's as valid a template for living life as any other. The resulting whirlwind of opinion in the middle isn't always fun to be in, mind, but maybe it drives processes which ripple their cause and effect outwards into a wider system we can't yet see. It's certainly stimulating us... This doesn't mean next time I see some stupid hoaxer on the telly that I'll be thanking him for raising the public profile of crop circles once again and creating some good old educational conflict, but we can at least rest easy that out of all this maelstrom, something positive, on some level, whenever, *WILL* come. Whether an answer will ever come is another matter. Quite possibly not. But there is a beauty to mystery.

While you're waiting for those elusive answers, don't forget to keep a sense of humour about it all. Have a laugh too, even as you take the subject seriously, and make the very most of this amazing phenomenon while you can - certainly, some of the glyphs have shown a sense of humour. Some even see the whole thing as one vast cosmic joke.

How long we will have the formations with us, no-one knows - I suspect only a few more years, if you want my *opinion*, before the curve of all this moves on to something else, or turns downward again, leaving the wildly elaborate, stunningly beautiful crop formations an obscure, strange curiosity of the late 20th, early 21st Century. Will it be a footnote in history, or a whole chapter? Maybe you will help decide that. Your vote counts.

Some who have been steeped in cerealogical upbringings are inevitably going on to pursue their own new avenues of investigation and understanding, or moving away to pastures new, sometimes into other subjects far beyond. Indeed, surely one of the lessons from the circles is that we should take what we have learnt from this phenomenon and apply it to other areas of life which need equal attention, whilst never losing affection for those glyphs which first fired us up.

There's a whole world of wonders out there just waiting to be explored - do it on an informed basis with compassion, discernment and integrity, avoiding second-hand opinions, and you can't go too wrong. A simple sci-fi television programme, *Doctor Who*, was one of my first childhood obsessions, so you'll forgive me for ending with the very last phrase from the very last episode of the series...

"There are worlds out there where the sky is burning, and the sea's asleep, and the rivers dream. People made of smoke and cities made of song. Somewhere there's danger, somewhere there's injustice, somewhere else the tea's getting cold. Come on, we've got work to do."

Enough said.

Original article: SC, issue 94, Spring 2001

APPENDIX A

Other books by Andy Thomas

Vital Signs:

A Complete Guide to the Crop Circle Phenomenon and Why it is NOT a Hoax

***Vital Signs* has been widely described as the definitive guide to the crop circle phenomenon.**

The book is currently available in a fully revised and updated 2002 edition, published by S B Publications in the UK, and Frog Ltd in the USA.

What are crop circles? Where and when do they appear? What could be *making* them? What strange effects surround them? What do they mean? Why is it many formations simply cannot be hoaxes? With over 200 colour and black and white photographs, *Vital Signs* is the ultimate guide to crop circles for newcomers and an essential summary for those already entranced, including the most complete chronological account of the crop circle mystery available.

Vital Signs has a foreword by award-winning film director and long-time crop circle enthusiast MIKE LEIGH (*Secrets and Lies, Topsy Turvy*, etc.), and was nominated for *Kindred Spirit* magazine's 2002 awards.

FOR DETAILS, EXTRACTS AND ONLINE ORDERING FOR THE UK EDITION OF *VITAL SIGNS* (**ISBN: 1-85770-256 -5**) AND OTHER BOOKS BY ANDY THOMAS, GO TO:

www.vitalsignspublishing.co.uk

Or write to: Vital Signs Publishing, 13 Downsview Cottages, Cooksbridge, East Sussex, BN8 4TA.

TO ORDER THE USA EDITION (**ISBN: 1-58394-069 -3**), GO TO:

www.northatlanticbooks.com

Or write to: North Atlantic Books, PO Box 12327, Berkeley, CA 94712

A Oneness of Mind:

The Power of Collective Thought and Signs of Our Times

A new book based on transcripts from Andy Thomas's renowned and illuminating Glastonbury presentations.

If you have enjoyed *Swirled Harvest*, you may also like to read *A Oneness of Mind.*

For almost a decade, Andy Thomas has been delivering lectures at the annual Glastonbury Symposium. Famed for his lively and theatrical presentations, Andy has increasingly moved beyond the crop circle subject to explore the wider issues of the power of collective consciousness and the global and personal responsibility that comes with it.

A Oneness of Mind is based on edited transcripts from Andy's performances between 1998 and 2002 and makes up an astonishing and controversial volume covering many inspirational topics:

Positive Living and the Negative World
Armageddon and How to Avoid it
Conspiracy and How to Live With it
Power and How we Give it Away
World War Three and Other Non-Events

With a foreword by acclaimed author and dowser Hamish Miller, *A Oneness of Mind* is a valuable record for those who have enjoyed Andy Thomas's Glastonbury lectures over the years, and essential reading for anyone with an interest in positively shaping the future of our world...

APPENDIX B

Useful References

SELECTED READING (A-Z by authors):

Crop Circle Year Books, Steve Alexander & Karen Douglas, Temporary Temple Press 1999 onwards, 28pp

Crop Circles: Exploring the Designs & Mysteries, Werner Anderhub & Hans Peter Roth, Lark Books, 2002, 144pp

Crop Circles: Harbingers of World Change, ed. Alick Bartholomew, Gateway 1991, 192pp

Patterns of Consciousness, Allan Brown, Dog's Press 2003

Ciphers in the Crops, ed. Beth Davis, Gateway 1992, 88pp

Circular Evidence, Pat Delgado & Colin Andrews, Bloomsbury 1989, 190pp

Crop Circles, Michael Glickman, Wooden Books 2000, 58pp

The Deepening Complexity of Crop Circles, Dr Eltjo Haselhoff, Frog Ltd. 2001, 157pp

The Cosmic Connection, Michael Hesemann, Gateway 1996, 168pp

Mysterious Lights and Crop Circles, Linda Moulton Howe, Paper Chase Press 2000, 342pp

Crop Circles: The Hidden Form, Nick Kollerstrom, Wessex Books 2002, 64pp

Crop Circle Geometry, John Martineau, Wooden Books 1992 onwards, varied pages

The Circles Effect and its Mysteries, George Terence Meaden, Artetech 1989, 116pp

The Face & the Message, John Michell, Gothic Image 2002, 36pp

Crop Circles Revealed, Judith Moore and Barbara Lamb, Light Technology Publishing 2001, 265pp

The Crop Circle Enigma, ed. Ralph Noyes, Gateway 1990, 192pp

Crop Circles: The Greatest Mystery of Modern Times, Lucy Pringle, Thorsons 1999, 144p

Secrets in the Fields, Freddy Silva, Hampton Roads 2002, 334pp

Fields of Mystery, Andy Thomas, S B Publications 1996, 100pp

Quest for Contact, Andy Thomas & Paul Bura, S B Publications 1997, 144pp

Vital Signs: A Complete Guide to the Crop Circle Mystery and Why it is NOT a Hoax, Andy Thomas, S B Publications (Frog Ltd in USA) 1998, revised 2002, 192pp

An Introduction to Crop Circles, ed. Andy Thomas, Wessex Books 2003, 48pp

The Secret History of Crop Circles, Terry Wilson, CCCS 1998, 155pp

CROP CIRCLE JOURNALS:

THE CEREOLOGIST: Global Circles Research, 17 Spindle Road, Norwich, Norfolk, NR6 6JR, UK

THE CIRCULAR: Centre for Crop Circle Studies, Kemberley, Victoria Gardens, Biggin Hill, Kent, UK

THE CIRCULAR REVIEW: 6D Pond View, Moor Farm, Moor Lane, Calverton, Nottinghamshire, NG14 6FZ, UK

CROP CIRCLES COMMENTARY: CCCS USA Network, 20075 SW Imperial Street, Aloha, Oregon 97006, USA

MEDWAY CROP CIRCULAR: Medway Crop Circle, 87 Hurstwood, Chatham, Kent, ME5 0XH, UK

THE SPIRAL: Wiltshire Crop Circle Study Group, PO Box 2079, Devizes, Wiltshire, SN10 1US, UK

SELECTED WEBSITES:

SWIRLED NEWS: http://www.swirlednews.com

Swirled News, edited by the author of this book, Andy Thomas, is the web site to access for informed news and reviews on the latest happenings and discoveries in the world of crop circles, supported by incisive and frank commentary, analysis, opinion and humour.

CROP CIRCLE CONNECTOR: http://www.cropcircleconnector.com

CROP CIRCLE RESEARCH: http://www.cropcircleresearch.com

INVISIBLE CIRCLE: http://invisiblecircle.de/uk

TEMPORARY TEMPLES: http://www.temporarytemples.co.uk

BLT RESEARCH: http://www.bltresearch.com

THE GLASTONBURY SYMPOSIUM: http://www.glastonburysymposium.co.uk

SOUTHERN CIRCULAR RESEARCH PUBLIC MEETINGS

Each month, SCR gathers at Burgess Hill, West Sussex, UK, to hear the latest crop circle news and views with slides, videos and guest speakers in a lively and friendly atmosphere. All meetings are open to the public.

Summer meetings between June and September are entertaining updates of all the latest crop circle events with slides, videos and animated discussion! Spring and autumn dates are a mix of the latest news and a special guest speaker. After each meeting, we move to *The Potter's* pub for drinks and chat.

Burgess Hill is easy to get to by road or rail, and is only 40 minutes train journey from London Victoria or London Bridge. We meet at:

THE SCOUT CENTRE, STATION ROAD, BURGESS HILL, WEST SUSSEX

Entrance is just opposite *The Potter's* pub. Meetings held in the upstairs room at 8.00pm sharp. There is a modest admission charge.

For details of travel directions and SCR meeting dates go to **http://www.swirlednews.com/meeting.asp**

Or e-mail: **info@swirlednews.com**

Or write to: **SCR, 13 Downsview Cottages, Cooksbridge, East Sussex, BN8 4TA, UK**

APPENDIX C

List of Uncaptioned Colour Plates and Diagrams

FRONT COVER MAIN PHOTO: 'Griller' Gilgannon gets down to some serious research, West Overton, Wiltshire, July 1993. Photo: Andy Thomas

FRONT COVER INSET PHOTOS (from top to bottom):
Roundway, Wiltshire, 31 July 1999. Photo: Frank Laumen
Cherhill, Wiltshire, 18 July 1999. Photo: Frank Laumen
West Kennett, Wiltshire, 4 May 1998. Photo: Andrew King
Alton Barnes, Wiltshire, 9 July 1998. Photo: Werner Anderhub

BACK COVER MAIN PHOTO: Conference closing ceremony, Alton Barnes, Wiltshire, July 1998. Photo: Andy Thomas

DIAGRAMS (by Allan Brown, unless otherwise stated):

INDEX

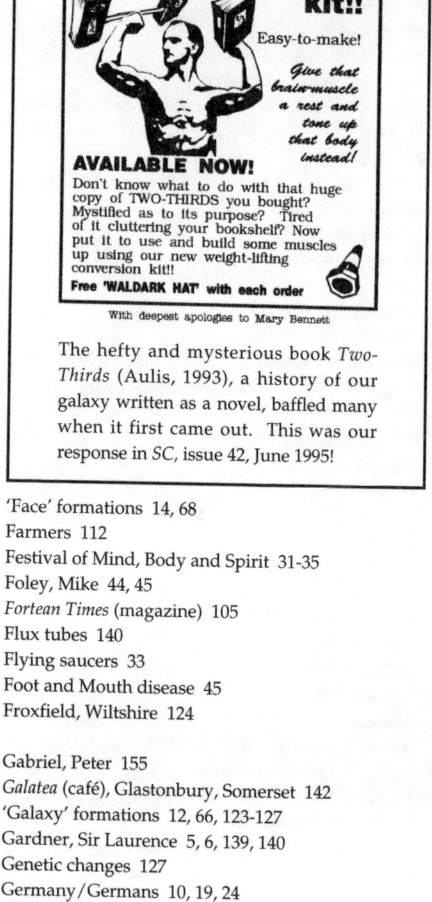

The hefty and mysterious book *Two-Thirds* (Aulis, 1993), a history of our galaxy written as a novel, baffled many when it first came out. This was our response in *SC*, issue 42, June 1995!

Even by 1995, the curse of hoax-claimants Doug and Dave refused to go away, as their story inexplicably enjoyed a resurgence in the media. Here was our take on it, with a nod to a certain Oliver Stone movie...
SC, issue 39, March 1995

THE AUTHOR

Andy Thomas is a founder member of the Southern Circular Research team (SCR), which carries out much active cerealogical work and has been holding regular public meetings since 1991. Andy is editor of the popular website *www.swirlednews.com*, renowned for its outspoken and insightful reporting. He previously produced *SC*, the globally-read bimonthly crop circle journal.

Andy has written three previous books exploring aspects of the crop circle enigma. *Fields of Mystery: The Crop Circle Phenomenon in Sussex* was the first in 1996, followed by *Quest For Contact: A True Story of Crop Circles Psychics and UFOs* in 1997 (with Paul Bura), which recounted some of the extraordinary experiences of the SCR team in their attempts to interact with the phenomenon. His best-known and much-praised book *Vital Signs: A Complete Guide to the Crop Circle Mystery and Why it is NOT a Hoax* (1998, revised 2002) has been described by many as the definitive guide to the subject.

Andy has provided forewords and contributions for several books, and written articles for many publications, including *Nexus Magazine*. He is also author of two books about his historical home town of Lewes, *Streets of Fire* (1999), and *The Lewes Flood* (2001).

A prolific lecturer, Andy is famed for his lively and sometimes theatrical presentations on crop circles and other inspirational topics. He has spoken extensively in England, and more recently in Europe and America. He is currently one of the organisers and presenters of the world's longest-running international annual crop circle conference, *The Glastonbury Symposium*, a three-day event held each summer in Somerset, England.

Andy has made numerous radio and TV appearances, including UK television spots on BBC 2's *Esther*, ITV's popular breakfast show *GMTV* and Channel 4's *Richard and Judy*. He has also featured in many overseas programmes from countries including America, Japan and Germany, and appeared in several crop circle documentary videos.

Also a professional keyboard player, Andy has composed and recorded for various projects in years past, and gigs around south-east England with guitarist Phil Light.

Andy Thomas can be contacted through Swirled News/SCR (see Appendix B).